Feb. 2016

Algonquin Area Public Library District
3 1488 00652 7022

Summer Bridge™

EXPLORATIONS

CARSON-DELLOSA
PUBLISHING GROUP

Greensboro, NC 27425 USA

Algonquin Area Public Library
2600 Harnish Dr.
Algonquin, IL 60102
www.aapld.org

D1401459

Caution: Exercise activities may require adult supervision. Before beginning any exercise activity, consult a physician. Written parental permission is suggested for those using this book in group situations. Children should always warm up prior to beginning any exercise activity and should stop immediately if they feel any discomfort during exercise.

Caution: Before beginning any food activity, ask parents' permission and inquire about the child's food allergies and religious or other food restrictions.

Caution: Nature activities may require adult supervision. Before beginning any nature activity, ask parents' permission and inquire about the child's plant and animal allergies. Remind the child not to touch plants or animals during the activity without adult supervision.

The authors and publisher are not responsible or liable for any injury that may result from performing the exercises or activities in this book.

Summer Bridge™
An imprint of Carson-Dellosa Publishing LLC
PO Box 35665
Greensboro, NC 27425 USA
carsondellosa.com

© 2015, Carson-Dellosa Publishing, LLC. The purchase of this material entitles the buyer to reproduce worksheets and activities for classroom use—not for commercial resale. Reproduction of these materials for an entire school or district is prohibited. No part of this book may be reproduced (except as noted), stored in a retrieval system, or transmitted in any form or by any means (mechanically, electronically, recording, etc.) without the prior written consent of Carson-Dellosa Publishing LLC.

Printed in the USA • All rights reserved.

ISBN 978-1-4838-1315-8

01-117151151

Table of Contents

© Carson-Dellosa

Table of Contents (continued)

© Carson-Dellosa

About *Summer Bridge Explorations*™

Summer Bridge™ Explorations includes a variety of resources to prevent learning loss and keep your child thinking, doing, and creating throughout the summer. Practice pages review skills your child learned in first grade and preview second grade skills. Throughout, you'll find instructions for completing real-world explorations that encourage your child to actively explore the outdoors, use imagination, and apply skills. Find these resources inside:

- **Three sections that correspond to the three months of a traditional summer vacation**
  Each section begins with an introduction that describes the monthly theme and explains the two real-world explorations your child can choose to complete.

- **Real-world explorations**
  Six hands-on projects connect real-life learning with summer fun. Your child will keep learning alive by applying new skills as he explores the world, close to home and on the road. Look for these symbols beside step-by-step instructions for completing each exploration.

   Treasure Hunt   Exercise Journal

   Trip Planner   Adopt an Animal

   Summertime Song   Summer Adventures Picture Book

- **Learning activity pages**
  Age-appropriate activities include phonics, writing, counting, addition and subtraction, telling time, learning about shapes, and more. Activities become progressively more challenging as the summer continues. Each month, help your child choose practice pages to build skills and support explorations.

- **Character development and fitness activities**
  Throughout each section, quick activities offer fun ways to think about values, exercise the body, and build strength and fitness inside and out.

- **Bonus science experiments and activities, social studies exercises, and outdoor learning experiences**
  These fun and creative activities are found in each section. Encourage your child to complete them as time allows.

- **Answer key**
  An answer key at the back of the book helps your child check her work.

© Carson-Dellosa

Fitness and Character Development

Throughout *Summer Bridge™ Explorations*, you and your child will find fun and easy ways to build strong character and a healthy body. These activities encourage your child to think about values and to get fit by focusing on three essential components.

Flexibility

Using and stretching the muscles and joints regularly allows us to accomplish everyday tasks easily, like bending to tie a shoe. Challenge your child to set a stretching goal for the summer, such as practicing daily until he can touch his toes.

It is also important to be mentally flexible. Talk with your child about how disappointing it can be when things don't go your way. Explain that by being flexible, we can choose how we react to circumstances and "make lemonade" when life gives us lemons. Respecting the differences of others, sharing, and taking turns are all ways for your child to practice mental flexibility.

Strength

Your child may think that only people who can lift heavy weights are strong. Explain to your child that she is strong, too. Point out how much stronger she has become since she was a toddler. Many summer activities build strength, such as carrying luggage, riding a bike, swimming, and playing outdoor games.

Inner strength allows us to stand up for what we believe, even when others do not agree. Your child can develop this important character trait by being honest, helping others, and putting her best efforts into every task.

Endurance

Aerobic exercise strengthens the heart and helps blood cells deliver oxygen to the body more efficiently. This summer, limit screen time for your child and encourage him to build endurance by jumping rope, playing tag, hiking, or playing basketball.

Having mental endurance means sticking with something, even if it is difficult. Look for times when your child is growing frustrated or bored with an activity this summer. He may be reluctant to continue swim lessons, baseball practice, or reading a longer book. Whatever it is, encourage him to stay with the task in order to reap the rewards.

© Carson-Dellosa

Index of Skills

Skill	Practiced on Pages	Skill	Practiced on Pages
Addition	5, 7, 10, 14, 19, 23, 27, 30, 34, 41, 46, 48, 49, 56, 64, 76, 80, 83, 88, 100, 103, 132, 139, 145, 147, 157, 160, 171, 173, 188, 190, 194, 201, 209	Place Value	20, 58, 91, 93, 96, 108, 150, 162, 167
Alphabet	5, 7	Planning & Organization	3–4, 9, 38, 51, 65–68, 74–75, 107, 112, 143–144, 151, 200
Character Development	46, 70, 76, 85, 102, 110, 145, 178, 201, 216	Problem Solving	14, 19, 34, 88, 103, 132, 145, 165, 193, 208, 210
Collecting & Representing Data	4, 6, 24, 36, 44, 52, 74–75, 109, 133, 195	Reading Comprehension	12, 20, 32, 42, 57, 63, 81, 84, 89, 92, 105, 111, 115, 120–121, 130–131, 146, 158–159, 168, 174–175, 183, 186, 187, 192, 196, 206–207, 209
Fine Arts	170, 176–177, 184–185, 197, 199, 211–212	Research	73, 87, 111, 113
Fitness	4, 19, 27, 38, 47, 60, 127, 145, 178	Science	16, 28, 39, 86, 98, 140, 156, 169
Grammar & Language Arts	8, 12, 26, 30, 33, 35, 37, 41, 48, 49, 59, 61, 62, 69, 78, 82, 88, 94, 95, 100, 101, 106, 108, 119, 121, 131, 148, 153, 163, 165, 173, 178, 180, 183, 189, 193, 194, 202, 207, 208	Shapes & Geometry	22, 29, 31, 33, 35, 37, 77, 79, 90, 95, 146, 148, 161, 163, 179, 182, 202
Handwriting	5, 7	Social Studies	15, 40, 53, 85, 97, 109, 123, 155, 215
Measurement	59, 61, 114, 117, 118, 125, 153, 164, 181, 189, 192, 204–205	Spelling	152, 162, 166, 179
Nature & Outdoors	54, 124, 169, 197, 198	Subtraction	5, 7, 10, 14, 19, 25, 27, 30, 34, 56, 58, 64, 76, 91, 94, 99, 100, 122, 160, 167, 188, 190, 193, 194, 203, 209
Numbers & Counting	11, 13, 17, 18, 45, 93, 96, 101, 102, 104, 106, 108, 126, 134, 164, 180, 191	Time & Money	17, 18, 21, 125, 127, 129, 132, 149, 152, 154, 165, 191, 193, 210
Patterns	43, 50, 126, 166, 180	Vocabulary	77, 79, 116, 118, 126, 128, 181, 187, 188, 190, 191
Phonics	8, 10, 13, 18, 21, 23, 25, 31, 34, 43, 45, 50, 55, 64, 78, 83, 91, 93, 103, 114, 122, 132, 147, 149, 157, 159, 160, 161, 172, 175	Writing	11, 26, 47, 48, 51, 55, 60, 61, 65, 69, 96, 101, 104, 108, 119, 128, 134, 135–138, 149, 154, 167, 182, 183, 194, 199–200, 210, 211–214

© Carson-Dellosa

Encouraging Summer Reading

Literacy is the single most important skill that your child needs to be successful in school. The following list includes ideas for ways that you can help your child discover the great adventures of reading!

- Establish a time for reading each day. Ask your child about what he or she is reading. Try to relate the material to a summer event or to another book.

- Let your child see you reading for enjoyment. Talk about the great things that you discover when you read.

- Create a summer reading list. Choose books from the reading list (pages ix–x) or head to the library and explore. To choose a book, ask your child to read a page aloud. If he or she does not know more than five words on the page, the book may be too difficult.

- Read newspaper and magazine articles, recipes, menus, maps, and street signs on a daily basis to show your child the importance of reading informational texts.

- Choose a simple book that contains dialogue to read with your child. Read one character's words yourself and have your child read (or act out) another character's words. Speak in a voice that suits your character. Discuss the different points of view the two characters may have.

- Choose a nonfiction book to read or reread with your child. Then, have him or her pretend to be a TV reporter, sharing the "news" of the book you read. Encourage your child to relate details and events from the story in the report.

- Make up stories. This is especially fun to do in the car, on camping trips, or while waiting at the airport. You can also have your child start a story and let other family members build on it.

- Encourage your child to join a summer reading club at the library or a local bookstore.

- Choose a favorite folktale or fairy tale. At the library, search for versions by different authors or from different cultures. Discuss the message or the moral of the story.

- Look through a nonfiction book with your child. Point out text features—including headings, captions, and diagrams—that help the reader understand.

© Carson-Dellosa

Summer Reading List

The summer reading list includes fiction and nonfiction titles. Experts recommend that students entering the fourth grade read for at least 20 to 30 minutes each day. Ask your child questions about the story to reinforce comprehension.

Fiction

Cannon, Janell
Stellaluna

Cooney, Barbara
Miss Rumphius

Cummings, Pat
Clean Your Room, Harvey Moon!

Eastman, P. D.
Are You My Mother?

Fox, Mem
Wilfrid Gordon McDonald Partridge

Gannett, Ruth Stiles
My Father's Dragon

Gerstein, Mordicai
How to Bicycle to the Moon to Plant Sunflowers: A Simple but Brilliant Plan in 24 Easy Steps

Hesse, Karen
Come On, Rain!

Hoban, Russell
A Bargain for Frances

Hoffman, Mary
Amazing Grace

Hoose, Phillip M.
Hey, Little Ant

Joyce, William
The Fantastic Flying Books of Mr. Morris Lessmore

McCloskey, Robert
Blueberries for Sal

McLerran, Alice
Roxaboxen

Nolan, Dennis
Dinosaur Dream

Polacco, Patricia
Fiona's Lace

Rylant, Cynthia
When I Was Young in the Mountains
Night in the Country

Say, Allen
Emma's Rug

Sendak, Maurice
Pierre: A Cautionary Tale in Five Chapters and a Prologue

Seuss, Dr.
Horton Hatches the Egg

Steig, William
Doctor De Soto
Sylvester and the Magic Pebble

Stevens, Janet
Tops & Bottoms

© Carson-Dellosa

Summer Reading List (continued)

Fiction (continued)

Titus, Eve
Anatole

Ungerer, Tomi
Fog Island

Woodson, Jacqueline
This Is the Rope: A Story from the Great Migration

Nonfiction

Aliki
Ah, Music!

Bang, Molly
Ocean Sunlight: How Tiny Plants Feed the Seas

Branley, Franklyn M.
The Big Dipper
What Makes Day and Night

DK Publishing
Eye Wonder: Bugs

Ehlert, Lois
The Scraps Book: Notes from a Colorful Life

Gove, Doris
My Mother Talks to Trees

Heiligman, Deborah
Jump into Science: Honeybees

Gibbons, Gail
Sunken Treasure

Larson, Kirby; Nethery, Mary
Two Bobbies: A True Story of Hurricane Katrina, Friendship and Survival

Leedy, Loreen
Look at My Book: How Kids Can Write and Illustrate Terrific Books

Markel, Michelle
Clara and the Shirtwaist Makers' Strike of 1909

McGovern, Ann
…If You Sailed on the Mayflower in 1620

Perrin, Clotilde
At the Same Moment, Around the World

Pfeffer, Wendy
Wiggling Worms at Work

Rockwell, Lizzy
The Busy Body Book: A Kid's Guide to Fitness

Showers, Paul
Where Does the Garbage Go?

Yaccarino, Dan
The Fantastic Undersea Life of Jacque Cousteau

© Carson-Dellosa

Section I Introduction

Theme: Learning in the Neighborhood

This month's explorations can be done close to home. They encourage your child to pay attention to his own actions each day and to consider ways to apply learning as it happens. This type of personal connection to information helps solidify knowledge and inspires children to seek out new learning experiences. Summer is a great time for your child to explore and experience the world nearby. Whether searching for insects in the yard or at the park, attending a farmers' market or community festival, or taking a walk around the block, you will find many opportunities to help your child observe and learn.

To build language arts and literacy skills this month, ask your child to find words all around—on street signs, ads for yard sales and other events, and products at the store. Encourage her to use phonics skills to read unfamiliar words and to notice variant spellings of similar sounds, such as the long *a* sound in *paint*, *cage*, and *may*. To practice writing skills, your child may like to write a neighborhood newsletter, prepare menus for a special picnic or barbeque, or create directions for a new game to play outside with friends.

To build math skills this month, look all around for ways to use math. Let your child select and weigh a certain number of fruits at the market, count out coins to pay for an ice cream cone, or add up scores during a family game. While exploring nature, encourage your child to notice the number of legs on an insect, patterns in flower petals, or how many birds at a feeder belong to the same species.

Explorations

This month, your child will have a choice of two explorations. He may choose to follow steps for one or both. Review the explorations below with your child and help him make a choice. Emphasize that it is useful to have a path in mind from the start. Then, help your child find and complete the project activities according to his plan. Throughout the section, your child will see the icons shown below on pages that include directions directly related to one of the explorations. Emphasize that breaking a large project into smaller steps helps make it fun and easy to do.

 **Treasure Hunt**

With this exploration, your child will put her first-grade skills to the test! The end goal is to design a clue-based treasure hunt for a friend. As your child reviews skills throughout the month, she will choose and create questions that would work well as clues to get the treasure hunter from point A to point B. This type of planning involves both critical thinking and creativity in addition to an understanding of the content. Your child will

© Carson-Dellosa

analyze questions for the types of answers they generate and choose those whose answers work well as clues. She will think creatively about how an answer could be used to get the treasure hunter from point A to point B, and she will craft directions that make it clear to the reader what to do next.

To help your child make meaningful connections with the skills he's practicing, encourage him to look for ways to apply those skills to the world around him. Discuss real-life addition and subtraction problems as they present themselves. Maybe that means figuring out how many tables will be needed at the block party or how many more packages of flour you need to buy for your baking extravaganza. For language arts, practice sounding out words you see around town, talk about causes and effects of everyday actions, and share opinions about stories and articles. The more learning has a purpose that's obvious to your child, the more fun it will be!

 **Exercise Journal**

This exploration's focus is math and fitness! Your child will practice data collection, graphing, and organization while staying active. Throughout the month, your child will keep track of all the ways she gets exercise. In addition to things like swimming, running the bases, or playing tag with friends, she might also be carrying groceries or walking up flights of stairs. She should write down anything she does that serves as exercise. Later in the month, she will add something new to her repertoire, and she will finish the month by creating a week-long exercise schedule.

To increase interest in exercise, help your child to understand the connection between staying active and being healthy and happy. Share your own experiences of relieving stress or just having fun by exercising. If you don't already, see if you can find some physical activities, like walking or hiking, to do regularly with your child.

It may be challenging at first for your child to collect data. To help her stay on track, you might set a time at the end of each day to record activities. You might also talk about the muscles you're using as you do everyday activities like climbing stairs, washing dishes, or walking to the corner market.

Learning Activities

Practice pages for this month review skills your child learned in first grade. They also focus on skills that support the explorations described above. Preview the activities and choose several that target skills your child needs to practice. Also select several relating to the exploration(s) your child plans to complete. You may wish to mark those pages with a star or other symbol to let your child know to begin with those. Then, let your child choose practice activities that interest her and allow her to demonstrate her growing skills.

© Carson-Dellosa

Treasure Hunt, Step I

Put your skills to the test! In this exploration, you will use what you learned last school year to design a treasure hunt. After reviewing your first-grade skills, you will hide a "treasure" somewhere around your house and then write clues to lead someone to it. Each clue will lead to the next, and the last clue will lead to the treasure.

To get started, think about the types of questions that would work as clues. You want to ask things that will get your treasure hunter to move from one place to another. Questions with numbers for answers work well. For example, if you want your treasure hunter to take 10 steps, you could ask, "What is 20 minus 10?" There are other ways to get someone from place to place, too. You could ask about the setting of a story and send the treasure hunter to a similar spot in real life. You could have the treasure hunter look for a particular shape based on its features (e.g. "Find the shape that has three sides that you can see from the backyard.") or find an object from its definition (e.g. "Go to the place that is attached to the house and has a roof but no walls.") See how many different ways you can come up with to get your treasure hunter moving!

In the box, list as many different kinds of questions as you can think of. Be creative and have fun!

© Carson-Dellosa

Exercise Journal, Step I

Summer is an active time. This month, keep track of the kinds of exercise you get. Are you swimming, jumping rope, running the bases, shooting basketball, or playing tag? What about carrying groceries or walking up the stairs? Keep track of what you do and how often you do it. Then, add something new to your "routine."

To get started, make an exercise chart. Put on the chart any physical activity you do on a regular basis. As the month goes on, you can add new exercises or ones you didn't think of. As you do each exercise, make a tally mark on the chart. (See the tally chart on page 6 for guidance.) Continue on a separate sheet of paper, if needed.

Name of Exercise	Number of Times

© Carson-Dellosa

Add or subtract to solve each problem.

1. $5 + 2 =$ _____

2. $9 - 3 =$ _____

3. $10 - 1 =$ _____

4. $3 + 4 =$ _____

5. $6 + 2 =$ _____

6. $8 - 5 =$ _____

7. $9 - 5 =$ _____

8. $8 + 2 =$ _____

9. $7 - 3 =$ _____

10. $8 - 4 =$ _____

11. $5 + 5 =$ _____

12. $6 + 3 =$ _____

13. $10 - 8 =$ _____

14. $7 - 6 =$ _____

15. $4 + 5 =$ _____

Write the capital letters of the alphabet.

AB

© Carson-Dellosa

Use the data from the table to answer the questions.

	Knights	Dukes	Guards	Counts	Jesters
King Ludwig	卌 卌 I	卌 IIII	卌 卌 卌 卌 卌 卌 卌 卌 II	卌 卌 卌 I	卌 卌 II
King Jonas	卌 III	卌 II	卌 卌 卌 卌 I	卌 卌 III	卌 卌 卌 卌 卌 I

1. How many knights and dukes does King Jonas have? _____

2. How many more guards does King Ludwig have than King Jonas? ___

3. How many guards and jesters does King Ludwig have? _____

4. Who has 28 dukes and guards combined? _____

5. Which king has fewer counts and jesters combined? _____

6. Who has fewer knights? _____

© Carson-Dellosa

Complete each fact family.

1. Family: 1, 4, 5

$1 + 4 = \boxed{}$

$4 + \boxed{} = 5$

$5 - 1 = \boxed{}$

$\boxed{} - 4 = 1$

2. Family: 3, 7, 10

$7 + 3 = \boxed{}$

$\boxed{} + 7 = 10$

$10 - \boxed{} = 3$

$10 - \boxed{} = 7$

3. Family: 4, 5, 9

$5 + 4 = \boxed{}$

$\boxed{} + \boxed{} = 9$

$9 - \boxed{} = \boxed{}$

$\boxed{} - 4 = \boxed{}$

Write the lowercase letters of the alphabet.

a b

CHARACTER CHECK: Today, when a family member asks you to do something, repeat the request to show you were listening. Example: "Okay, I'll put my toys away."

© Carson-Dellosa

Circle the word that matches each picture.

1. 　　　bog　　　　　dog　　　　　hog

2. 　　　star　　　　　far　　　　　car

3. 　　　bat　　　　　bit　　　　　bet

4. 　　　peg　　　　　pug　　　　　pig

Read each sentence. Circle each noun. A noun can be a person, place, or thing.

5. The smallest child won the race.

6. The red wagon was full of toys.

7. Did Cara share her candy?

8. Our neighbors have a trampoline.

9. Andy rode his new bike today.

© Carson-Dellosa

Treasure Hunt, Step 2

It's time to gather the facts for your treasure hunt! Return to your list of question types on page 3. As you review your math and language arts skills, be on the lookout for questions that match the types on your list. Be open to other kinds of questions, too. Remember, you want to use questions that have clear answers that could take your treasure hunter one step closer to the treasure. Either copy questions directly from the workbook, or change them into what works for you. Include the answers, too—check the answer key to make sure your answers are correct.

© Carson-Dellosa

Complete each fact family.

1. Family: 4, 3, 7

   4 + 3 = ☐

   3 + 4 = ☐

   7 − 3 = ☐

   7 − 4 = ☐

2. Family: 6, 3, 9

   6 + ☐ = 9

   3 + ☐ = ☐

   9 − ☐ = 3

   9 − ☐ = ☐

3. Family: 3, 5, 8

   ☐ + ☐ = ☐

   ☐ + ☐ = ☐

   ☐ − ☐ = ☐

   ☐ − ☐ = ☐

Say the name of each picture. Write the letter of each long vowel sound.

4.  _____

5.  _____

6.  _____

7. 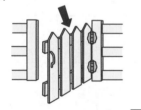 _____

8.  _____

9.  _____

FACTOID: Snakes do not have eyelids.

© Carson-Dellosa

Write > or < to compare each set of numbers.

1. 17 ◯ 13

2. 93 ◯ 83

3. 51 ◯ 75

4. 49 ◯ 26

5. 31 ◯ 27

6. 78 ◯ 87

7. 21 ◯ 19

8. 73 ◯ 38

9. 46 ◯ 94

10. 14 ◯ 29

11. 62 ◯ 26

12. 98 ◯ 78

13. 88 ◯ 100

14. 54 ◯ 65

15. 50 ◯ 49

Think of three ways to finish this sentence. Write your sentences on the lines.

I like my best friend because . . .

16. _____

_____ .

17. _____

_____ .

18. _____

_____ .

© Carson-Dellosa

Read each noun in the box. Write it in the correct column.

Dogwood Elementary	weekend	mall
peanut	Ms. Crios	sister
Marcus	Wednesday	

Common Nouns	**Proper Nouns**
_____	_____
_____	_____
_____	_____
_____	_____

Read each sentence. Draw a picture of your favorite sentence.

The dog chased the squirrel.

The girl hit the ball out of the park.

The boy raced his dad home.

The baby hugged her teddy bear.

The woman splashed in a puddle.

© Carson-Dellosa

Count the tens. Write each number. The first one is done for you.

1. 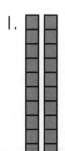 __20__

2. 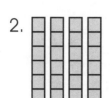 _____

3. 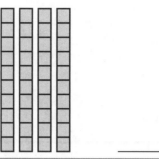 _____

4. 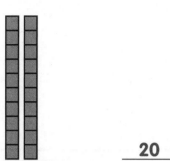 _____

5.  _____

6. 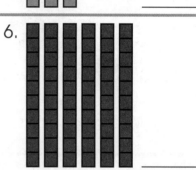 _____

Say the name of each picture. Write the letter of each vowel sound.

7. 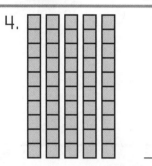 r _____ ke

8.  f _____ n

9. 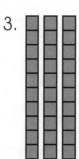 dr _____ m

10.  f _____ x

11.  ch _____ n

12.  m _____ ce

© Carson-Dellosa

Add or subtract to solve each problem.

1. There are 8 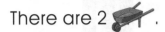.

   There are 2 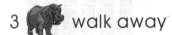.

   What is the sum? _____

---

2. There are 6 .

   3 walk away

   What is 6 minus 3? _____

---

3. I have 4 .

   I buy 4 more .

   How many do I have now? _____

---

4. Ivan has 2 .

   Helen has 5 .

   How many more does Helen have? _____

---

5. There are 7 .

   3 more come.

   How many in all? _____

© Carson-Dellosa

Make a Map

Look closely at this photograph of an old pioneer schoolhouse and playground.

Directions:

In the box, draw a map to show what is in the photograph. Use the shapes to help you draw the pictures on your map that stand for things in the photo.

Pioneer Map

© Carson-Dellosa

BONUS

Liquid Motion

Some liquids have more molecules than others. **Speed** is the term used to describe how fast an object moves. Try this experiment to see if the same object moves through different liquids at the same speed.

Materials:
- two identical jars
- two identical marbles
- water
- vegetable oil
- stopwatch that measures to 0.1 or 0.01 seconds
- ruler

Procedure:
1. Fill one jar with water and one jar with vegetable oil. Make sure the same amount of liquid is in each jar.
2. Hold the marble so the bottom of it touches the top of the vegetable oil.
3. Drop the marble.
4. Use the stopwatch to record the time in seconds that it takes the marble to reach the bottom of the jar.
5. Use the ruler to measure the distance the marble travels.
6. Follow the same procedure for the second marble and the jar of water.

Which marble traveled faster? _____

What is the difference between the speed of the first marble and the speed of the second marble?

_____

© Carson-Dellosa

Complete each number line.

Count by tens.

1.

0 _____ 20 _____ _____ _____

Count by fives.

2.

5 _____ 15 _____ _____ 30

Write the time shown on each clock.

3.

_____ : _____

4.

_____ : _____

5.

_____ : _____

6.

_____ : _____

FACTOID: The biggest clock face in the world is more than 141 feet wide!

© Carson-Dellosa

Look at each picture. Write the letters of the beginning and ending sounds.

1.
____ **e** ____

2.
____ **o** ____

3.
____ **o** ____

4.
____ **u** ____

5.
____ **e** ____

6.
____ **ea** ____

When you count nickels and dimes, you count by fives and tens. Count the coins, and write the total amount on the line.

7.
____ ¢

8.

____ ¢

9.
____ ¢

10.

____ ¢

18

© Carson-Dellosa

Add or subtract to solve each problem.

1. Ms. Jackson has 5 dogs and 4 cats. How many pets does she have in all?

2. Mr. Black has 8 black labs and 3 poodles. How many more black labs than poodles does he have?

3. Mr. Zucker has 8 terriers. Five are boys, and 3 are girls. How many more boys than girls are there?

4. Ms. Nimm has 4 black labs and 4 yellow labs. How many labs does she have combined?

5. Mr. Kelly has 2 adult beagles and 8 beagle puppies. How many beagles does he have total?

6. Ms. Miller's oldest dog is 9 years old, and her youngest is 6 years old. What is the difference in their ages?

Fast Clap

See how fast you can clap your hands. Set a timer for 30 seconds. First, hold your hands in front of you. See how many claps you can do in 30 seconds. Next, reset timer, and hold your hands above your head. Was it harder to clap in this position? Finally, set the timer again, and clap with your hands behind your back. Now, how many times did you clap? Were you using different muscles?

© Carson-Dellosa

Count the tens and ones. Write each number. The first one is done for you.

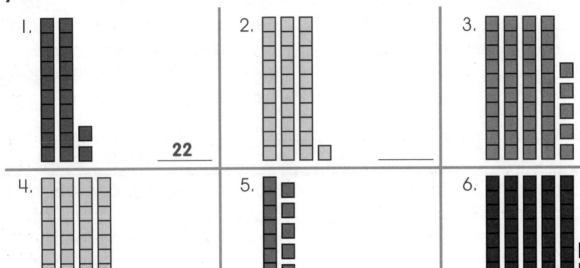

1. _22_

2. _____

3. _____

4. _____

5. _____

6. _____

Draw a line to match each sentence with the correct job.

EXAMPLE:

I save people from burning buildings.   librarian

7.   I help people get well.   chef

8.   I cook meals.   firefighter

9.   I drive children to school.   nurse

10. I help people find books.   bus driver

11. I help keep people safe.   police officer

© Carson-Dellosa

Write the correct time for each clock that has hands. Draw hands on each clock that has a time below it.

1.

5:30

2.

____ : ____

3.

9:30

4.

____ : ____

5.

11:00

6.
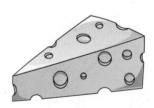

____ : ____

Say the name of each picture. Circle the letters that make each beginning sound.

7.

ch   wh   sh

8.

qu   wh   sh

9.

ch   wh   sh

© Carson-Dellosa

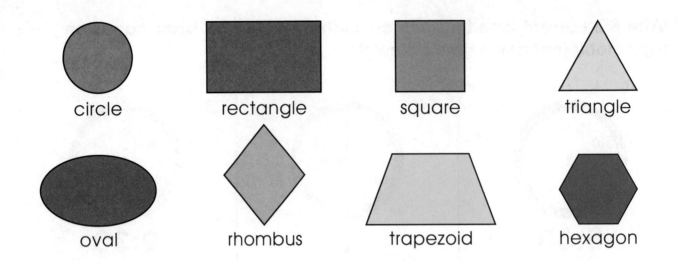

circle rectangle square triangle

oval rhombus trapezoid hexagon

Color the shapes to match the shapes at the top of the page.

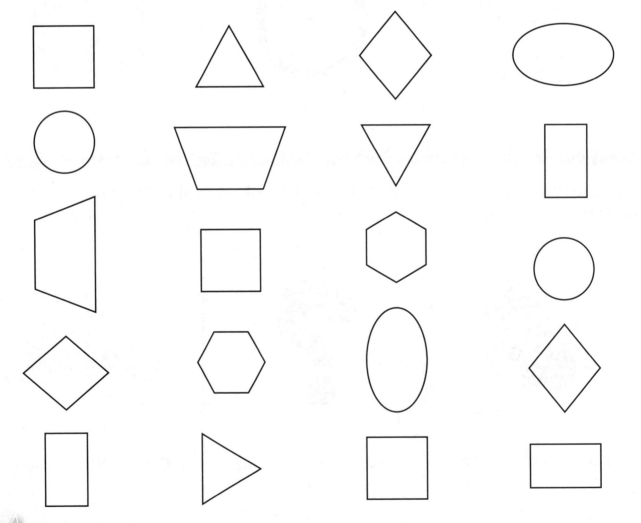

© Carson-Dellosa

Read each word. Circle the words in each row that rhyme with the first word.

1.	**cat**	tap	hat	rat	man
2.	**fan**	can	sun	pan	jam
3.	**hop**	mop	pot	top	pop

Add to find each sum. Use the ten frames for help.

4.
$$15$$
$$+\ \ 1$$

5.
$$11$$
$$+\ \ 4$$

6.
$$13$$
$$+\ \ 3$$

7.
$$16$$
$$+\ \ 4$$

FACTOID: In 2013, a man hopped a mile on one foot in just 23 minutes and 15 seconds!

© Carson-Dellosa

Use the picture graph to answer the questions.

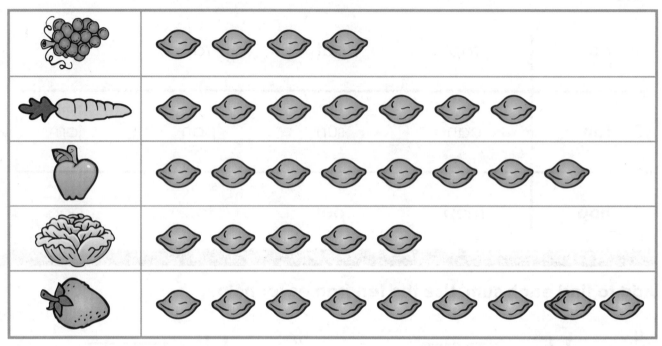

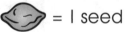 = 1 seed

1.   How many grape seeds are there? _____

2.   How many carrot seeds are there? _____

3.   Which plant has 9 seeds? _____

4.   How many more apple seeds are there than lettuce seeds? _____

5.   How many strawberry and apple seeds are there? _____

6.   Which plant has the fewest seeds? _____

7.   How many more carrot seeds than grape seeds are there? _____

8.   How many apple and carrot seeds are there in all? _____

© Carson-Dellosa

Read each word. Circle the words in each row that rhyme with the first word.

1.	**leap**	jeep	leaf	keep	eat
2.	**cake**	bake	rate	lake	bait
3.	**feet**	eat	meet	seat	Pete

Subtract to find each difference. Use the ten frames for help.

4.
$$20 - 5$$

5.
$$13 - 3$$

6.
$$18 - 2$$

7.
$$16 - 5$$

FITNESS FLASH: Sit in a chair, place your right ankle just above your left knee, and bend forward to stretch. Hold for 20 seconds and then switch legs.

© Carson-Dellosa

Some pronouns tell who owns something or who belongs to whom. Write a word from the box to replace each word in bold type.

her	my	his	their

1. **Mason's** birthday = _____ birthday

2. **Radna** and **Rae's** mother = _____ mother

3. **Lari's** crayons = _____ crayons

4. the bike **belonging to me** = _____ bike

Fill in each blank. Ask an adult if you need help.

The best thing about first grade was _____

_____.

I learned _____, _____, and

_____. My teacher was _____.

If you are going into first grade, you should _____

_____

_____.

FACTOID: A child in first grade in the U.S. would be in "year two" in England.

© Carson-Dellosa

Math Fact Leapfrog

Practice your math facts with a friend while playing leapfrog!

- First, decide together how high you want to go with your facts (example: 1–20) and whether you will practice addition, subtraction, or both.

- Then, take turns leaping over each other. To start, crouch on the ground, like in the picture below. Then, call out a number—such as "6"—to start your math equation.

- Your friend then puts his hands on your back, and leaps over you. While doing this, he says either "plus" or "minus."

- After your friend leaps over you, he crouches down, and then you leap over him. As you leap, say the second number in the equation.

- Your friend will then leap over you one last time and say "equals" and the answer to the problem.

- Take turns starting equations so that both players have a chance to solve them.

© Carson-Dellosa

BONUS

Counting Beats

As you exercise, try charting your pulse rate. Use your index or pointer finger and your middle finger to take your pulse. Encourge everyone in your family who is exercising to fill out a chart, too.

Directions:
  1. Give each person a copy of the pulse rate chart.
  2. When you are ready to begin, have one person sit still. Find his/her pulse and start counting the beat for one minute. The timer watches the second hand of a clock or watch and says "Stop" after 60 seconds. Record the rate on the chart after the date and under the column marked **Before Exercise**. Do the same for everyone else.
  3. Next, exercise. **After exercise**, take pulses as you did in Step 2. Mark charts.
  4. Cool down by walking around slowly for one minute. Then, repeat Step 2 and record the pulse rate under **Recovery** on the same line.
  5. Repeat three more times on three other dates.

Name:			
Date	Before exercise	After exercise	Recovery

© Carson-Dellosa

Draw each shape based on its description. Then, name the shape.

1. This closed shape has 4 equal sides and no slanted lines.

   Shape: _____

2. This closed shape has 3 sides.

   Shape: _____

3. This closed shape has no sides and is perfectly round.

   Shape: _____

4. This closed shape has six equal sides.

   Shape: _____

REMINDER: Are you keeping track of all the types of exercise you're doing? Make sure to make a tally mark on page 4 each time you do a particular type.

© Carson-Dellosa

Add or subtract to solve each problem. Use the number line to help you.

| 0 | 1 | 2 | 3 | 4 | 5 | 6 | 7 | 8 | 9 | 10 | 11 | 12 | 13 | 14 | 15 | 16 | 17 | 18 | 19 | 20 |

1.   3
    + 9

2.   7
    + 7

3.   16
    − 5

4.   12
    − 4

5.   6
    + 5

6.   8
    + 8

7.   19
    − 7

8.   20
    − 3

9.   14
    + 2

10.   10
     + 5

11.   18
     − 9

12.   11
     − 4

13.   9
     + 6

14.   13
     + 7

15.   20
     − 10

Underline the present-tense verb to complete each sentence.

16.   Marla (left/leaves) for swim class in five minutes.

17.   We (hopped/hop) on the bus when it arrives.

18.   Please (turn/will turn) the lights off.

19.   Do you (wanted/want/will want) to go to the soccer game?

© Carson-Dellosa

Say the name of each picture. Write **1** if the word has one syllable.
Write **2** if the word has two syllables.

1.

_____

2.

_____

3.

_____

4.

_____

Draw the shape you have when you put the following shapes together.

5.

6.

7.

8.

© Carson-Dellosa

**One of the characters below fits all of the clues in the poem.
Circle the character.**

Who's there? Was that the breeze? Or is something hiding behind those trees?

Who's there? The light is dim, but I don't think that you will swim.

Who's there? Did you hear me call? You don't look so very small.

Who's there? Can you fly? I see a tail going low and high.

Who's there? Come along! I see four legs, big and strong.

Who's there? Should I give you space? I see whiskers on your face.

Who's there? No, don't come back! I don't want to be your snack.

© Carson-Dellosa

Draw lines to show how you and a friend can equally share each item. The first one is done for you.

1.

2.

Draw lines to show how you and 3 friends can equally share each item.

3.

4.

Rewrite each sentence with a past-tense verb.

5. Clarice jogs to school.

    _____

6. Zach washes the car.

    _____

7. Sema sings beautifully.

    _____

© Carson-Dellosa

Solve each problem.

1. There are 20 .

   There are 8 .

   What is the difference? _____

2. There are 7 on the table.

   There are 6 in the drawer.

   How many in all? _____

Read each word. Then, find a word in the box that has the same long-vowel spelling. Write it on the line.

tie	goat	tweet	flow	day	peach

3. tree _____

4. team _____

5. float _____

6. pie _____

7. bow _____

8. play _____

© Carson-Dellosa

Choose the correct name of each 3-D shape.

1. cone   square   cube

2. rectangular prism   cylinder   cube

3. triangular prism   cone   sphere

4. cylinder   rectangular prism   cone

For each sentence, write the future tense form of the verb given in parentheses.

5. Tomorrow, we (leave) _____ for vacation.

6. Our neighbor (take) _____ our picture once the car is loaded.

7. When we get to the hotel, Mom (check) _____ us in.

8. I (put) _____ on my bathing suit right away.

9. My brother (cheer) _____when he sees the swimming pool.

10. The next morning, we (go) _____to the amusement park.

REMINDER: How many clues have you written for your hunt? Make sure you have both language arts and math questions.

© Carson-Dellosa

Use the bar graph to answer the questions.

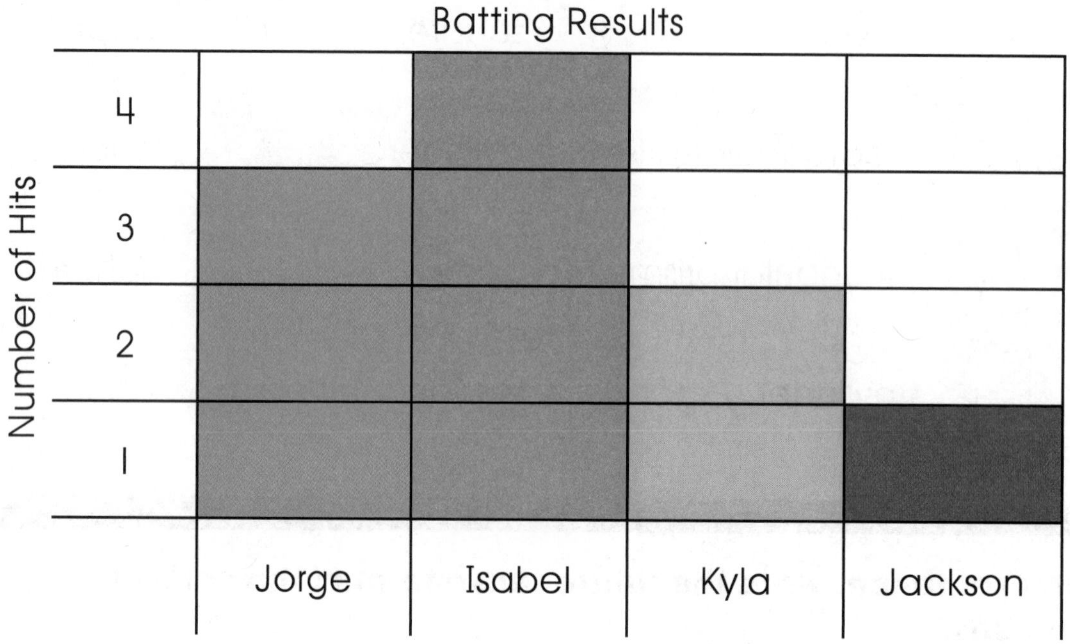

Batting Results

	Jorge	Isabel	Kyla	Jackson

(Number of Hits: 1–4)

1. Who got the most hits? _____

2. Who got the fewest hits? _____

3. Who got one hit less than Isabel? _____

4. How many hits did Jorgé and Jackson get altogether? _____

5. How man hits did the children get in all? _____

FITNESS FLASH: Lie down, stretch your arms above your head, and roll 10 times.

© Carson-Dellosa

Add a verb to each subject to make a simple sentence.

1. The tiny brown puppy _____.

2. Julie and Damara _____ outside.

3. The red and white airplane _____.

4. Bees _____ around the flowers.

Draw the shape you have when you put the following shapes together.

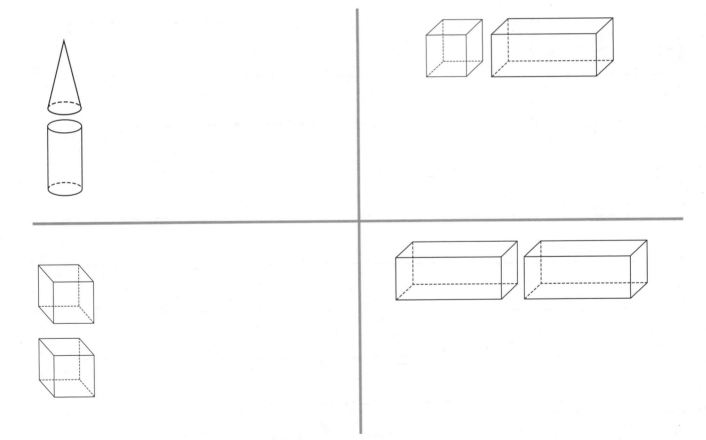

CHARACTER CHECK: What is something you are grateful for? Tell a friend or family member about it.

© Carson-Dellosa

Exercise Journal, Step 2

Have you been keeping track of your exercises this month? Great! Now, it's time to add something new. Look at your exercise chart on page 4. Which exercises are the most fun? Highlight those and think about what makes them fun for you.

Then, use the box below to brainstorm ideas for a new fun way to be active. It could be an exercise you know about but haven't tried, a new version of a game like tag, or just a way to use your arm muscles while you walk the neighborhood.

After you've listed at least five ideas, choose your favorite one, and add it to the chart on page 4.

© Carson-Dellosa

In the Blink of an Eye

Did you know that people blink about once every 5 seconds? We blink in order to cleanse our eyes and keep them from drying out.

But, not everyone blinks the exact same number of times. The number of blinks varies from person to person and from situation to situation.

Test this out. Observe friends and family members of different ages. Try to watch some people indoors and some people outdoors. Using a stopwatch or a timer, record how many times each person blinks per minute. Are the numbers similar? Record your observations below.

Name	Blinks per Minute

What do you notice about the data you collected? Did older and younger people blink at different rates? Did it seem to matter whether someone was indoors or outdoors? Do you think the number of blinks would change if it was a windy day? What about if the air was dusty or smoky?

© Carson-Dellosa

Symbols Replace Words

Symbols on a map show you where things are located.

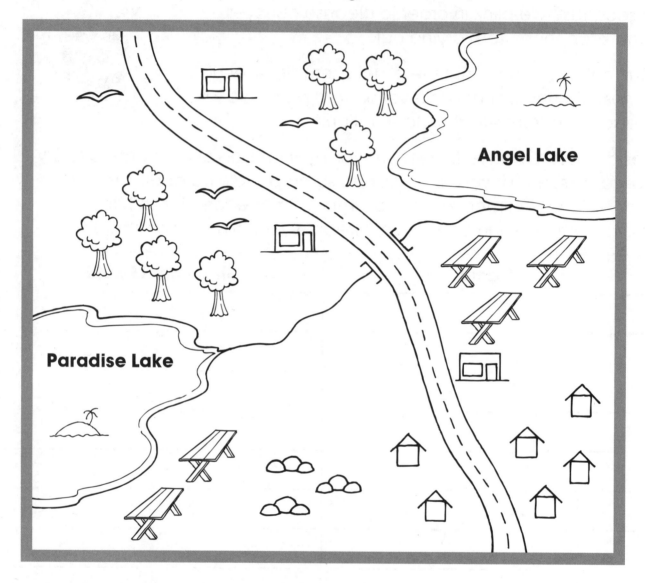

Use crayons or markers to complete the map.

1. Color the islands brown.
2. Color the trees green.
3. Color the rocks black.
4. Color the houses blue.
5. Color the stores orange.
6. Color the birds purple.
7. Color the picnic tables red.
8. Color the road yellow.

© Carson-Dellosa

When you add three digits together, first add the first two numbers. Then, add the last number. Use this method to find each sum below. The first one is done for you.

1. 2
    7 → 9
    + 4 + 4
         13

2. 4
    5
    + 2

3. 7
    2
    + 1

4. 2
    3
    + 7

5. 7
    2
    + 6

6. 8
    4
    + 5

7. 9
    1
    + 4

8. 8
    7
    + 2

Combine each pair of sentences into a compound sentence. Use the conjunction in parentheses ( ). Make sure to put a comma before each conjunction.

EXAMPLE: Carter cleared the table. He didn't wash the dishes. (but)
   Carter cleared the table, but he didn't wash the dishes.

9. Janelle climbed the jungle gym. Audra went down the slide. (and)

    _____

10. After lunch, Patrick rides his bike. He plays with friends. (or)

    _____

11. Mom saw the sand on our shoes. She knew we had been at the beach. (so)

    _____

12. The dog sprinted across the park. Its owner sat down on a bench. (but)

    _____

© Carson-Dellosa

Read the story below. Then, answer the questions.

Rebecca and Neela

Rebecca and Neela are best friends. They have the same haircut. They wear the same clothes. They love to read. Both girls have their own pet. Rebecca has a bird. Neela has a mouse. Rebecca lets her bird, Jade, fly around her room. Neela keeps her mouse, Julius, in his cage. Rebecca and Neela take good care of their pets.

1. What do Rebecca and Neela love to do? _____

2. How do the girls look alike? _____

   _____

3. In the picture, what is one thing that is different about the girls? _____

   _____

   _____

4. How do they play differently with their pets? _____

   _____

© Carson-Dellosa

Continue each pattern by drawing 3 more pictures.

1.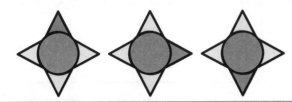

2.

3.

Say the name of each picture. Write the letters for the blend at the beginning of each word. In a blend, like sl in slide, two consonants make a sound together.

4.

    _____ _____

5.

    _____ _____

6.

    _____ _____

7.

    _____ _____

8.

    _____ _____

9.

    _____ _____

FACTOID: Frogs never close their eyes, not even when they sleep!

© Carson-Dellosa

Skyler and his family went to the zoo. They saw 5 monkeys, 3 tigers, 4 giraffes, and 2 elephants. Color the graph to show how many of each animal Skyler's family saw.

Zoo Animals

Skyler's family saw more _____ than any other animal.

© Carson-Dellosa

Say the name of each picture. Write the letters for the digraph at the beginning or end of each word. In a digraph, like sh in show, two consonants together make one sound.

1.  ___ ___	2.  ___ ___	3.  ___ ___
4.  ___ ___	5.  ___ ___	6.  ___ ___

Write > or < to compare each set of numbers.

7. 21 ◯ 23

8. 27 ◯ 20

9. 98 ◯ 89

10. 95 ◯ 77

11. 53 ◯ 41

12. 41 ◯ 22

13. 14 ◯ 18

14. 17 ◯ 29

15. 57 ◯ 76

16. 58 ◯ 65

17. 74 ◯ 39

18. 16 ◯ 44

19. 37 ◯ 28

20. 43 ◯ 100

21. 72 ◯ 81

© Carson-Dellosa

Add to find each sum. You may need to carry a 1 to the tens place. The first problem is done for you.

1.
$$\begin{array}{r} 1 \\ 38 \\ +\ 4 \\ \hline 42 \end{array}$$

2.
$$\begin{array}{r} 19 \\ +\ 6 \\ \hline \end{array}$$

3.
$$\begin{array}{r} 27 \\ +\ 5 \\ \hline \end{array}$$

4.
$$\begin{array}{r} 20 \\ +\ 6 \\ \hline \end{array}$$

5.
$$\begin{array}{r} 13 \\ +\ 4 \\ \hline \end{array}$$

6.
$$\begin{array}{r} 38 \\ +\ 8 \\ \hline \end{array}$$

7.
$$\begin{array}{r} 22 \\ +\ 6 \\ \hline \end{array}$$

8.
$$\begin{array}{r} 29 \\ +\ 3 \\ \hline \end{array}$$

9.
$$\begin{array}{r} 47 \\ +\ 2 \\ \hline \end{array}$$

10.
$$\begin{array}{r} 14 \\ +\ 1 \\ \hline \end{array}$$

11.
$$\begin{array}{r} 63 \\ +\ 5 \\ \hline \end{array}$$

12.
$$\begin{array}{r} 53 \\ +\ 6 \\ \hline \end{array}$$

13.
$$\begin{array}{r} 87 \\ +\ 2 \\ \hline \end{array}$$

14.
$$\begin{array}{r} 41 \\ +\ 4 \\ \hline \end{array}$$

15.
$$\begin{array}{r} 79 \\ +\ 9 \\ \hline \end{array}$$

Be Kind

How do you show kindness? Do you offer help when it's needed? Do you invite others to play with you and your friends? Think about a way you could be kind to another child. Draw a picture of what that would look like.

© Carson-Dellosa

Write a paragraph about your favorite exercise or physical activity. Give at least three reasons that this activity is your favorite.

_____

_____

_____

_____

_____

_____

_____

_____

_____

_____

_____

FITNESS FLASH: Jog in place for 30 seconds, lifting your knees as high as you can.

47

© Carson-Dellosa

Add to find each sum. You may need to carry a 1 to the tens place.

1.	63	2.	42	3.	29	4.	71	5.	62
	+ 6		+ 5		+ 9		+ 8		+ 3

6.	45	7.	19	8.	30	9.	16	10.	22
	+ 4		+ 6		+ 9		+ 7		+ 4

11.	30	12.	81	13.	47	14.	56	15.	48
	+ 6		+ 7		+ 2		+ 5		+ 7

Add to each simple sentence to make a compound sentence. Use the conjunction and, but, or, or so. Make sure to put a comma before the conjunction.

16.   Vanessa pitched the ball. _____

17.   Dad bought the broccoli. _____

18.   We wanted to jump rope. _____

19.   The car would not start. _____

© Carson-Dellosa

Write first, then, and last to show the order the pictures would happen in.

1.

_____   _____   _____

2.

_____   _____   _____

Add to find each sum.

3.   15
   + 10
	4. 19
	   + 20
		5. 23
		   + 20
			6. 31
			   + 10
				7. 47
				   + 20

8.   13
   + 30
	9. 29
	   + 40
		10. 17
		   + 40
			11. 11
			   + 50
				12. 60
				   + 30

13.   75
   + 10
	14. 50
	   + 40
		15. 25
		   + 70
			16. 42
			   + 50
				17. 12
				   + 80

© Carson-Dellosa

Say the name of each picture. Write the consonant blend at the beginning or end of each word. Choose from fl, gr, pl, sk, sm, and tr.

1.

_____

2.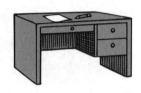

_____

3.

_____

4.

_____

5.

_____

6.

_____

Look at each pattern. Draw the shape to answer each question.

7. What will the eighth shape be?

_____

8. What will the tenth shape be?

_____

9. What will the next shape be?

_____

10. What will the seventh shape be?

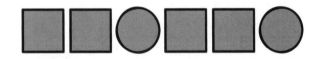

_____

© Carson-Dellosa

Treasure Hunt, Step 3

Now that you have questions in mind for your treasure hunt, it's time to plan the hiding places. First, decide where around the house or yard to hide your treasure. Make sure it's a good hiding place. You don't want your treasure hunter to be able to see the treasure at first glance.

Next, find places that would work well for hiding your clues. Then, decide which order to put those places in. Where will the treasure hunt start? Do you want the treasure hunter taking the longest possible route to each place? Do you want the places to be close together?

Once you have the order of places in mind, write clues that will lead to each place. Keep in mind that you want to ask questions that have answers you yourself know. For math problems, that may mean keeping numbers on the small side (which could affect how far apart each hiding place is). If it's helpful, draw a map that shows where you'll be hiding each clue.

Finally, choose questions from the list you wrote on page 9 and turn them into specific clues for your hunt. Write these on a separate sheet of paper. Keep in mind that it's not enough to ask the question. The treasure hunter needs to know what to do once he or she has the answer. Here are some examples of questions with directions for the treasure hunter:

- $12 + 6 =$ _____. Solve the problem and then walk that many paces to the south.
- Measure this dog bone using the paperclips provided. Walk that many paces west and then turn left.
- Go to the room with a name that has three syllables.
- What comes next in the pattern? Use that image as your clue.
- What is the main idea of this paragraph? Go to the person in my family who knows most about this topic.
- This shape has 6 faces and can be found on the kitchen counter. When you find this shape, look inside it.

© Carson-Dellosa

Exercise Journal, Step 3

Now, take the exercise data you've been collecting on page 4 and represent it in a bar graph. This will help you see more clearly which exercises you've done most and least. If you need help, revisit the bar graphs on pages 36 and 44. Use the blank graph below, or create your own. After graphing your exercises, answer the question that follows.

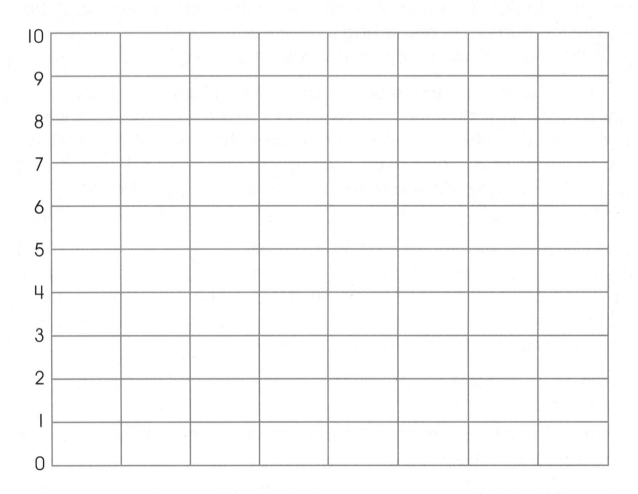

Is what you do the most for exercise also what you like the most? If not, make a change for the better.

© Carson-Dellosa

What You Need

People need certain things in order to stay healthy and safe. Circle the items below that are things people need, not just things they might want.

| cake | a home | food |

| an airplane | the Sun | water |

| a guitar | trees | jewelry |

© Carson-Dellosa

BONUS

Take It Outside!

You can use things you find outside to draw! Find several brightly colored things, like grass, leaves, and flower petals. Rub them on a white piece of paper to see the colors they leave behind. You might even try crushing softer rocks and mixing the dust with water to make a type of paint. Use your natural objects to make a picture. How are the natural colors different from the art supplies you usually use?

Find out what foods ants like best. Put several small pieces of food on a paper plate. You could try cereal flakes, carrot or cheese shavings, sugar, apple bits, or popcorn. Put the plate outside near a place where you have seen ants. Watch to see what the ants take. How many ants does it take to lift each piece? What do you notice about the way ants work?

Put an ice cube into each of two small bowls. Bring the bowls outside into the sun. Put a black piece of paper over the top of one bowl and a white piece of paper over the top of the other bowl. Check your bowls every few minutes. Which ice cube melted faster? Why do you think that is? Try the experiment a few more times with different colored paper. What do you notice?

© Carson-Dellosa

Write the word that matches each set of clues.

EXAMPLE:

It begins like <u>tr</u>uck.
It rhymes with s<u>nap</u>. _____

1. It begins like <u>st</u>ar.
    It rhymes with m<u>op</u>. _____

2. It begins like <u>f</u>og.
    It rhymes with s<u>it</u>. _____

3. It begins like <u>th</u>is.
    It rhymes with b<u>at</u>. _____

Write a paragraph for a younger brother, sister, cousin, or friend. Explain how to do something step by step. You could explain how to make a bed, ride a bike, or build a sand castle. Use sequence words like first, next, then, and last.

_____

_____

_____

_____

_____

_____

© Carson-Dellosa

Add or subtract to solve each problem.

1. 17 + 4	2. 18 + 2	3. 12 + 3	4. 20 + 1	5. 19 + 6
6. 14 + 10	7. 39 + 20	8. 42 + 30	9. 21 + 10	10. 18 + 30
11. 60 − 30	12. 30 − 30	13. 90 − 20	14. 70 − 40	15. 20 − 10
16. 80 − 50	17. 90 − 70	18. 50 − 20	19. 40 − 10	20. 80 − 60
21. 12 3 + 2	22. 10 5 + 5	23. 14 2 + 3	24. 8 9 + 1	25. 4 7 + 6
26. 3 2 + 1	27. 5 1 + 3	28. 4 4 + 2	29. 10 1 + 4	30. 11 2 + 2

CHARACTER CHECK: Do you always keep your promises? Why is it important to do what you say you'll do?

© Carson-Dellosa

Read the story. Then, follow the directions below.

Forest Animals

Many kinds of animals live in the forest. Some forest animals are very small. They have six legs. They are insects. Butterflies, ants, beetles, and bees are insects.

Some forest animals spend their entire lives in lakes or streams. They have scales. They breathe through gills. They are fish. Trout, bass, and catfish are fish.

Other forest animals are reptiles and amphibians. Amphibians spend part of their lives in the water and part of their lives on the land. Frogs and toads are amphibians. Snakes, lizards, and turtles are reptiles.

Look at the names of the animals in each list. Look at the titles in the box. Write the correct title on each line.

| Amphibians | Reptiles | Insects | Fish |

1. _____

   trout
   bass

2. _____

   frogs
   toads

3. _____

   butterflies
   bees

4. _____

   snakes
   lizards

© Carson-Dellosa

Write a paragraph describing what you see, hear, smell, and touch right now. Include what you taste, too, if appropriate.

_____

_____

_____

_____

_____

_____

Subtract to find each difference. Use the tens blocks for help.

1.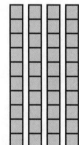
$$\begin{array}{r} 40 \\ -\ 30 \\ \hline \end{array}$$

2.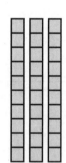
$$\begin{array}{r} 30 \\ -\ 20 \\ \hline \end{array}$$

3.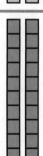
$$\begin{array}{r} 20 \\ -\ 10 \\ \hline \end{array}$$

4.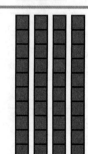
$$\begin{array}{r} 40 \\ -\ 20 \\ \hline \end{array}$$

© Carson-Dellosa

Write the correct punctuation mark at the end of each sentence. Use (.), (!), or (?).

1. This is the best day ever
2. The car is in the garage
3. Chickens cannot fly
4. Where is my coat
5. Is that your mom
6. Watch out
7. Why does water boil
8. You can ride your bike
9. Quick! Open the door
10. Glue the yarn to the paper

Use the paper clips to measure. Then, number the objects as follows: 1– long, 2 – medium, 3 – short.

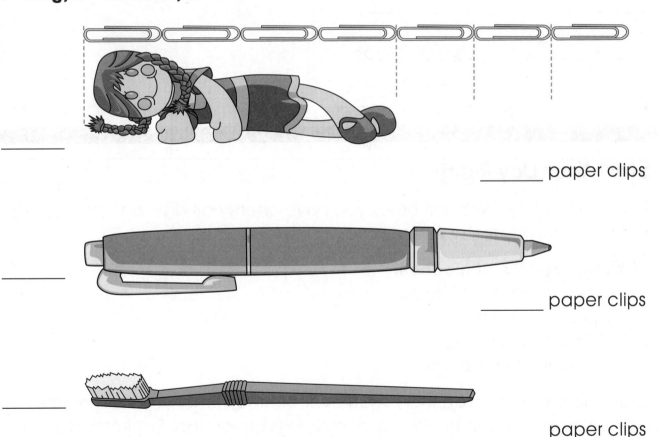

_____ _____ paper clips

_____ _____ paper clips

_____ _____ paper clips

FACTOID: Chickens can't fly, but they can swim if they have to!

© Carson-Dellosa

What do you think the perfect playground would look like? Desribe it and draw a picture of it.

_____

_____

_____

_____

_____

_____

_____

Start Your Day Right!

Eating a healthy breakfast helps you have energy all day, and that energy will help you stay fit. Try this fun and delicious recipe!

Yogurt and Pistachio Toast
2 slices whole-grain bread
4 TBS plain yogurt
2 TBS pistachio meats
2 tsp honey or maple syrup

Toast the bread. Spread the yogurt over the toast. Then, sprinkle on the pistachios and drizzle the honey or maple syrup on top. Eat immediately and smile!

© Carson-Dellosa

Follow the directions below.

1. Write a sentence that ends with a period (.).

    _____

2. Write a sentence that ends with a question mark (?).

    _____

3. Write a sentence that ends with an exclamation point (!).

    _____

Count how many cubes long each toy is. Write the number on the line.

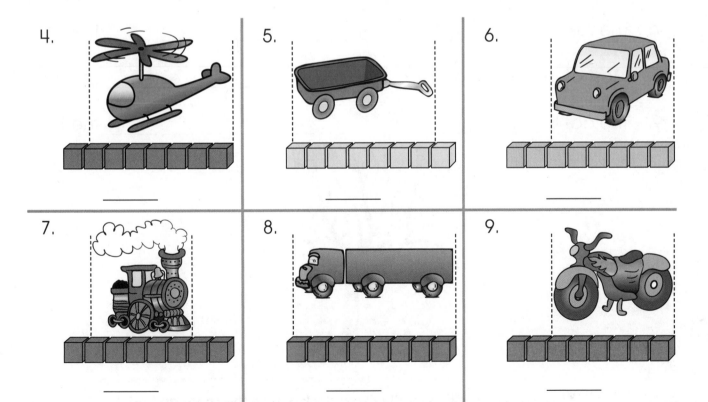

4. _____

5. _____

6. _____

7. _____

8. _____

9. _____

© Carson-Dellosa

Add the word parts. Write the new word on the line.

1. walk + ed = _____

2. bright + er = _____

3. un + button = _____

4. hand + ful = _____

5. re + name = _____

6. pre + test = _____

Write the word or phrase that tells where each object is. Use under, in, and next to one time each.

7. The rake is _____ the tree.

8. Most of the leaves are _____ the tree.

9. The cat is _____ the tree.

FITNESS FLASH: Waddle like a duck across the room and back.

© Carson-Dellosa

Read each paragraph. Read the sentences. Then, circle the main idea of each paragraph.

1. All insects have six legs. Butterflies and bees have six legs. They are insects. Spiders have eight legs. They are not insects.

    A. Spiders are not insects.

    B. Bees are insects.

    C. Insects have six legs.

2. Insects eat different things. Some insects eat plants. Caterpillars eat leaves. Bees and butterflies eat the nectar of flowers. Some insects eat other insects. Ladybugs eat aphids. Ant lions eat ants.

    A. Ladybugs eat aphids.

    B. Insects eat different things.

    C. Butterflies eat nectar.

3. Insects live in different kinds of homes. Bees build hives out of wax. Ants and termites build hills on the ground. Some insects, like mayflies and damselflies, live underwater. Other insects live under rocks or in old logs.

    A. Insects live in different kinds of homes.

    B. Some insects live underwater.

    C. Some insects build hills.

© Carson-Dellosa

Circle the word that names each picture.

1.
hear
hay

2.
paint
pant

3.
weed
wed

4.
bet
beet

5.
light
lit

6.
bean
ben

Add or subtract to solve each problem.

7.   12
    + 4

8.   18
    + 2

9.   25
    + 10

10.   27
    + 20

11.   33
    + 30

12.   70
    − 30

13.   60
    − 60

14.   30
    − 20

15.   50
    − 40

16.   80
    − 10

17.   11
     4
    + 1

18.   9
     6
    + 5

19.   13
     1
    + 2

20.   7
     8
    + 2

21.   3
     6
    + 5

FACTOID: The first paints were made from charcoal or dirt mixed with animal fat.

© Carson-Dellosa

Treasure Hunt, Final Step

Check the order of the clues you wrote after following the directions on page 51. You may need to adjust questions and answers slightly to get from point A to point B. If you're using a person to hold a clue, make sure that person either stays in one place during the hunt or holds a clue that doesn't need a particular starting point.

Next, choose a treasure to hide. Make it something fun but inexpensive. Maybe it's a sheet of stickers, a bouncy ball, or a cool pencil or eraser. Check with your parents that it's okay to give it away to a friend.

Then, write your clues on individual note cards or slips of paper. Make sure it's clear what the treasure hunter is supposed to do once he or she has the answer.

Finally, test your hunt on yourself and then on an adult. If everything works right, ask a friend to take the treasure hunt challenge. Make sure your treasure is in place!

© Carson-Dellosa

Treasure Hunt
Finished Product Example

Here is an example of how your treasure hunt might look if it was mapped out. To see how the clues lead to each other, read each one and follow the footprints.

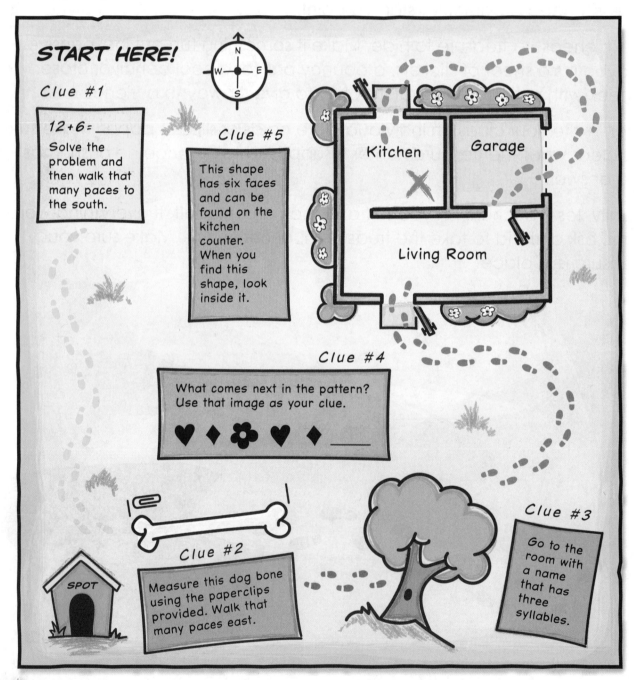

START HERE!

Clue #1

12 + 6 = _____
Solve the problem and then walk that many paces to the south.

Clue #5

This shape has six faces and can be found on the kitchen counter. When you find this shape, look inside it.

Kitchen

Garage

Living Room

Clue #4

What comes next in the pattern? Use that image as your clue.

♥ ◆ ❀ ♥ ◆ _____

Clue #3

Go to the room with a name that has three syllables.

SPOT

Clue #2

Measure this dog bone using the paperclips provided. Walk that many paces east.

© Carson-Dellosa

Exercise Journal, Final Step

You have kept track of your physical activities all month, and you've graphed them to see which ones you did the most. Now, choose the exercises you liked best and make a weekly exercise calendar for your wall! Follow the steps below.

Materials:

- your exercise chart on page 4 and your graph on page 52
- writing paper
- poster board
- markers
- ruler
- glitter and glue or other decoration (optional)

Directions:

1. Look back at your exercise chart on page 4 and your graph on page 52. Which activities were your favorites? Which did you do most often? Put a star next to the exercises that you know you will be able to do every week.

2. On a sheet of paper, write down the days of the week and two exercises you will do on each day. Try to do something different each day so that you don't get bored with your choices.

3. Draw a picture to represent each exercise.

4. Use a ruler to draw a week-long calendar on your poster board. (See the example on the next page.) Copy your exercises for each day onto the calendar. Include your drawings. You might even want to write how many times or for how long you'll do each exercise.

5. Give your calendar a name (for example, "Get Your Exercise!").

6. Decorate your poster using markers, glitter, and anything else that will draw your attention when you see it. You want your calendar to call out to you each day, reminding you to exercise.

7. See if you can follow your schedule for two full weeks! Then, if you want, change the exercises and make a whole new schedule.

© Carson-Dellosa

Exercise Journal
Finished Product Example

Here is an example of how your exercise calendar might look.

GET YOUR EXERCISE!

SUN	MON	TUE	WED	THU	FRI	SAT
Milk-jug curls	Jumping jacks	Cartwheels and forward rolls	Butterfly stretch	Hide-and-seek with neighbors	Dance with baby brother	Hiking with Mom and Dad
5 times each arm	20 times	20 minutes	20 minutes	3 minutes	30 minutes	? Hours
Stair steppers	Batting practice	Karate kicks	Jog around the block	Carry groceries	Frog squats	Pencil stretch and calf stretch
3 flights	30 minutes	10 times each leg	10 minutes	2-3 bags	20 times	5 minutes

© Carson-Dellosa

What's in a Name?

Be a poet, just by writing your name! Use the letters of your name to make a poem all about you.

STEP 1

Write your name in uppercase letters in the box. Then, think of a word that begins with each letter and also describes you. Write one word next to each letter of your name. If you want, you can write a group of words or even a whole sentence.

STEP 2

Now, on a separate sheet of paper, write your name in uppercase letters from the top to the bottom of the page. You may want to color the letters of your name to make them stand out. Then, next to each letter, add the rest of the word or phrase that goes with it.

Example:

Silly
Talented
Egg eater
Pie lover
Happy
Afraid of alligators
Not sleepy
Imagines
Everything

STEP 3

When you finish writing, decorate your poem in a way that represents you!

© Carson-Dellosa

Summer Fun Goal

What is one activity you would like to learn to do this summer? Think of a sport or hobby that would be fun for you to try. Then, plan how you will make it happen.

Summer Fun Goal:_____

What is the first step to reaching your goal?_____

_____

Who can you ask for help?_____

_____

What will be the easiest part for you?_____

_____

What will be the hardest?_____

_____

Draw a picture of yourself doing this activity.

© Carson-Dellosa

Section II Introduction

Theme: Travel and Learn

This month's explorations can be completed while traveling to places near and far. They encourage your child to build knowledge and make connections while visiting new and familiar places. Engage your child in family travel plans by looking at maps together, choosing destinations and activities, and reflecting on cultural experiences. Whether you travel to a family reunion, to a state or national park, or to another part of the world, you will find many opportunities to help your child learn during your adventures.

To build language arts and literacy skills this month, invite your child to help you use guidebooks, brochures, and websites to research travel destinations. Long car rides and waits at the airport are perfect opportunities to read books, tell stories, and play word games together. During your trip, purchase postcards and encourage your child to use them for writing simple messages to friends and relatives back home.

To build math skills this month, point out to your child the important role that numbers play when traveling. Mile markers, gallons of gasoline purchased, hours traveled, time zone changes, and admission prices to attractions all make great real-world math lessons. Use situations from your travel adventures to invent simple addition and subtraction word problems for your child to solve. During road trips, notice numbers on license plates of passing vehicles and use them for more math practice.

Explorations

This month, your child will have a choice of two explorations. He may choose to follow steps for one or both. Review the explorations below with your child and help him make a choice. Emphasize that it is useful to have a path in mind from the start. Then, help your child find and complete the project activities according to his plan. Throughout the section, your child will see the icons shown below on pages that include directions directly related to one of the explorations. Emphasize that breaking a large project into smaller steps helps make it fun and easy to do.

 **Trip Planner**

With this exploration, your child will develop research, writing, and organizational skills as she investigates a vacation spot. If you are taking a family trip this summer, let it become a meaningful learning experience for your child, even before you leave! If you are staying close to home, your child can research a place she would like to go someday. Either way, she will look into attractions, weather, and local or regional foods. Then, she will use her findings to design a brochure to encourage others to visit that vacation spot.

© Carson-Dellosa

Your child will need some guidance while researching online. Look for trusted tourism and weather websites, especially those featuring pictures. Alternatively, your child may enjoy looking through guidebooks and almanacs. There are some interesting travel guides written especially for children now. Although they cover fewer places than adult guides, your vacation spot might be one of them. However you guide your child in her research, help her see how much fun it is to explore a new place, even before arriving.

 **Adopt an Animal**

With this exploration, your child will develop science and writing skills by observing wildlife during summer adventures. He will keep track of animals he sees close to home and far away. For each type of animal, your child will write a simple description, take a photograph, or make a drawing. Your child will choose one animal from the list to adopt as a pet (only in his imagination, of course!). He will research what that animal eats, how much exercise it needs, and how to care for that animal as a pet. Finally, he will put together an "adoption request," showing how he will be a suitable caretaker for his chosen animal.

Again, your child will need some guidance as he searches for information. The Internet is a great place to start, but you will likely find plenty of books on wildlife and specific animals at the local library. Encourage your child to read wildlife books, non-fiction picture books, and articles about his chosen animal. Zoo websites are another source of information on caring for wild animals in captivity. Note: You may want to remind your child that the adoption request is just for fun and that, generally, wild animals do not make good pets.

Learning Activities

Practice pages for this month move from first grade review to an introduction of second grade skills. They also focus on skills that support the explorations described above. Preview the activities and choose several that target skills your child needs to practice. Also select several relating to the exploration(s) your child plans to complete. You may wish to mark those pages with a star or other symbol to let your child know to begin with those. Then, let your child choose practice activities that interest her and allow her to demonstrate her growing skills.

© Carson-Dellosa

Trip Planner, Step 1

Going somewhere this summer, or wish that you were? For this exploration, choose either a place you are planning to visit or a place you'd like to visit. Then, prepare for your trip! Before you go, you will design a travel brochure to share information that will get others excited about the trip, too.

Often, the most exciting part about visiting a place is its attractions. Attractions are fun or interesting things to see and do. What attractions does your vacation spot offer? Does your family have plans to visit museums, parks, beaches, mountains, or amusement parks? Find out about three attractions you could visit on your trip. Find a picture and basic information about each one.

If you search online, you may be able to print out the pictures that you find. Try the official travel and tourism sites for U.S. states as well as sites like the World Tourism Cities Federation. These often have great pictures of places to visit within particular cities. You could also head to your local library. There are many travel books written specifically for young people. Ask a librarian for help finding a book on your vacation spot.

Fill in the chart below with information about three attractions.

Attraction Name:	Attraction Name:	Attraction Name:
_____ _____	_____ _____	_____ _____
Location: _____ _____	Location: _____ _____	Location: _____ _____
Why to Go There: _____ _____	Why to Go There: _____ _____	Why to Go There: _____ _____

© Carson-Dellosa

Adopt an Animal, Step I

Have you ever imagined having a wild animal as a pet? This month, you will be on the lookout for wild animals you would like to adopt (for pretend, of course!). At the end of the month, you will research your chosen animal and make a case for bringing it home!

As you travel or explore your neighborhood, keep track of the animals you see. Each time you see an animal not on your list, write down its name or a description of it. Then, say what the animal was doing and anything else you noticed about it. Draw or take a picture of each animal. If you don't know the animal's name, your picture will help you find out.

Animal	What It Was Doing	What Else I Noticed

© Carson-Dellosa

Animal	What It Was Doing	What Else I Noticed

© Carson-Dellosa

Use each fact family to write two addition and two subtraction number sentences.

1.

14
9 5

__9__ + __5__ = __14__

_____ + _____ = _____

_____ − _____ = _____

_____ − _____ = _____

2.

11
4 7

_____ + _____ = _____

_____ + _____ = _____

_____ − _____ = _____

_____ − _____ = _____

3.

15
8 7

_____ + _____ = _____

_____ + _____ = _____

_____ − _____ = _____

_____ − _____ = _____

All About You

Make a list of all the things you like about yourself. Include things about your talents, your abilities, your personality, and your appearance. Read your list anytime you need a boost!

_____

_____

_____

_____

_____

© Carson-Dellosa

Complete.

1.

   There are ___2___ equal parts.

   ___1___ of the parts is shaded.

   ___1/2___ of the whole is shaded.

2.

   There are _____ equal parts.

   _____ of the parts is shaded.

   ___—___ of the whole is shaded.

Write the fraction that is shaded in words.

3.

   ___One-half___ is shaded.

4.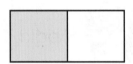

   _____ is shaded.

Circle the word that means the same as the bold word.

5. My mother bought me a **pretty** dress.

   old   beautiful   ugly

6. I cannot find my red baseball **cap**.

   hat   top   jacket

7. Since I'm not feeling well, I will **rest**.

   eat   play   sleep

8. My little brother loves to **jump** in mud puddles.

   hop   walk   run

© Carson-Dellosa

Circle the verb in each sentence.

1. Akiko placed her new puppy on the rug.

2. The puppy sniffed the rug and the couch.

3. The puppy ran in circles around the room.

4. Akiko giggled at the excited little dog.

5. The puppy chewed on Akiko's green slipper.

Circle the word that names each picture.

6. paid
    pad

7. rough
    right

8. cot
    coat

9. coast
    cost

10. beads
    beds

11. met
    meat

12. goat
    got

13. red
    read

14. tray
    train

FACTOID: Seventy-one percent of Earth's surface is covered by ocean.

© Carson-Dellosa

Complete.

1.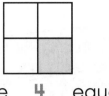

There are ___4___ equal parts.

___1___ of the parts is shaded.

$\frac{1}{4}$ of the whole is shaded.

2.

There are _____ equal parts.

_____ of the parts is shaded.

___—___ of the whole is shaded.

Write the fraction that is shaded in words.

3.

___One-fourth___ is shaded.

4.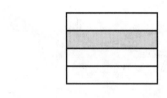

_____ is shaded.

Draw a line from each word on the right to the word on the left with the opposite meaning.

5. dark   night

6. day   finish

7. small   light

8. tall   big

9. start   short

Add to solve each problem.

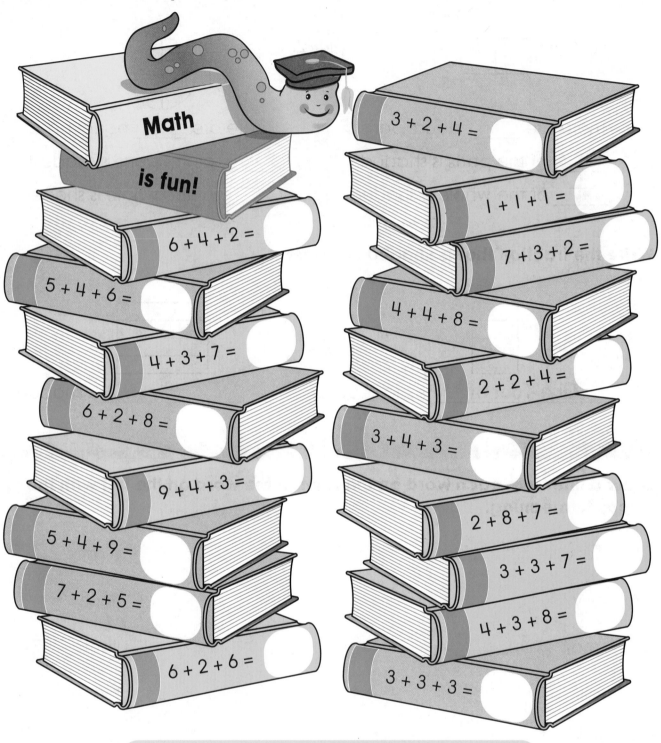

Math

is fun!

6 + 4 + 2 =

5 + 4 + 6 =

4 + 3 + 7 =

6 + 2 + 8 =

9 + 4 + 3 =

5 + 4 + 9 =

7 + 2 + 5 =

6 + 2 + 6 =

3 + 2 + 4 =

1 + 1 + 1 =

7 + 3 + 2 =

4 + 4 + 8 =

2 + 2 + 4 =

3 + 4 + 3 =

2 + 8 + 7 =

3 + 3 + 7 =

4 + 3 + 8 =

3 + 3 + 3 =

CHARACTER CHECK: Make a thank-you card
for someone who has done something nice for you.

© Carson-Dellosa

Write each title at the top of its matching story.

When Yang Yang Is Sick

Becoming a Zookeeper

The Panda Keeper

What Yang Yang Eats

1.

Brenda Morgan is a zookeeper in Washington, D.C. Brenda has the very important job of caring for a panda named Yang Yang at the zoo. She is in charge of making sure Yang Yang is happy and healthy.

2.

Brenda always wanted to work closely with animals and help care for them. As a child, Brenda wanted to be a horse when she grew up! Since she could not become a horse, she became a zookeeper instead. Brenda loves her job at the zoo.

3.

Part of Brenda's job is to watch Yang Yang closely to be sure he is feeling well. Once, he had an eye infection, and Yang Yang went blind for a few days. Brenda called the veterinarian for medicine, and now Yang Yang is well again.

4.

Yang Yang eats many kinds of foods. He likes gruel, which is made of rice, honey, and cheese. He also enjoys apples and bamboo. Brenda thinks his favorite food is carrots.

© Carson-Dellosa

Draw a line to match each contraction to its word pair.

EXAMPLE:

isn't   it is

1. it's   you are

2. we'll   did not

3. you've   we will

4. didn't   is not

5. you're   you have

Write the correct verb to complete each sentence.

6. The grass _____ beautiful.
                   is   are

7. I could _____ some juice.
                drink   drank

8. Amelia _____ a song.
                sing   sang

9. Chris _____ a new scooter.
              has   have

10. Did Charles _____ his bed?
               make   made

11. He _____ a race.
              run   ran

© Carson-Dellosa

Say each word in the box. Listen for the long vowel sound. Write the word under the correct heading.

muted	acorn	bedtime	Thursday	human
eagle	rider	argue	flavor	yellow
frozen	motion	unkind	reason	fever

Long a	**Long e**	**Long i**	**Long o**	**Long u**
_____	_____	_____	_____	_____
_____	_____	_____	_____	_____
_____	_____	_____	_____	_____

Add to find each sum. Draw a line to match each dog with the correct bone.

1. 32
    + 21

3. 44
    + 13

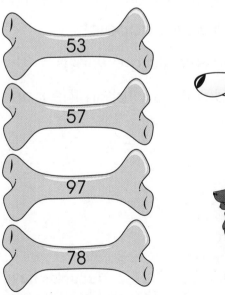

53

57

97

78

2. 73
    + 24

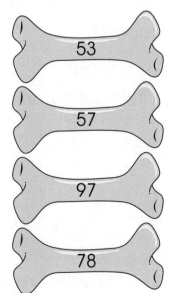

4. 52
    + 26

83

© Carson-Dellosa

Read each paragraph. Then, circle the main idea.

1. It was spring. The breeze was soft and warm. The grass on the hills was green. White clouds floated across the blue sky.

    A. The grass was green.

    B. The sky was blue.

    C. It was spring.

2. Noah went outside to play. His ball rolled near the fish pond. Noah had not looked at the pond since fall. He stopped to see the fish. There were four goldfish. There were also some new fish. They were small and dark. Noah ran back to his house to get his dad.

    A. Noah liked to play ball.

    B. Noah saw new fish in the pond.

    C. Noah had four goldfish.

3. Noah's dad came out to look at the new fish. He said they were not fish at all. He said they were tadpoles. He told Noah that the tadpoles would grow bigger and bigger. He said that in a month or two, they would grow legs. The tadpoles would grow up to be frogs.

    A. The new fish were tadpoles.

    B. The tadpoles would grow legs.

    C. Noah's dad put new fish in the pond.

FACTOID: Tadpoles have gills like fish so they can breathe underwater.

84

© Carson-Dellosa

Declare Your Independence!

On the Fourth of July, we celebrate our country's independence. Why not celebrate your own independence this month, too?

Think about what makes you uniquely you. What do you do that is different from what your friends do? What are some of your favorite games, hobbies, foods, and songs? What kinds of things do you think about when you are by yourself? What else makes you unique?

Now, draw yourself in three situations. Show the ways you are thinking or acting independently in each.

Feathered Friend Feeders

Materials:

- grapefruit halves
- cereal
- peanuts
- birdseed
- string or yarn
- stale bread
- peanut butter
- plastic knives
- cookie cutter shapes

Directions:

1. **Grazing Grapefruits**

   Start with half of an empty grapefruit skin. (Clean this beforehand and share the fruit if you like.) Poke three holes in the skin and thread three pieces of string through the holes. Tie them together so the grapefruit will be balanced when it hangs. Fill the grapefruit skin with nuts, cereal, or birdseed. Hang the bird feeders on a tree branch.

2. **Cookie Cutter Café**

   Cut a shape out of a slice of stale bread using a cookie cutter. Then, spread one side of the bread with peanut butter and sprinkle nuts or seeds onto the peanut butter until the bread is well coated. Next, carefully poke a small hole through the center of the bread and thread a piece of yarn through it. Hang the bird feeder in a tree to create a yummy café for your feathered friends.

Note:

Birds may become dependent on the feeder for their food supply. You should continue feeding the birds during the winter months when food may be scarce.

© Carson-Dellosa

Trip Planner, Step 2

Before you go on your trip, you need to know what to pack. Find out what the weather is like in your vacation spot this time of year. Is it sunny and warm? Does it rain a lot? Will there be snow? Search weather sites on the Internet and find out!

You can find the forecast for any major city in the world, even for a whole month, on the Internet. You can also find the average temperature of a place for each month. Ask an adult to help you search.

Write what the weather will be like in your vacation spot during the time you'll be there. Then, write what clothes you will need to pack to be ready for the weather.

Weather in my Vacation Spot:

_____

What to Pack:

_____

_____

_____

_____

_____

_____

© Carson-Dellosa

Write is or are to complete each sentence.

1. Where _____ my raincoat?

2. _____ he planning to help?

3. This book _____ not mine.

4. _____ you coming to my party?

5. We _____ going out for breakfast.

6. Seals _____ fast swimmers.

Solve each problem.

7. There are 22 students in one class. There are 24 students in the other class. How many students are there altogether?

8. Thomas saw 48 fish in one fish tank. Brooke saw 36 fish in another fish tank. How many fish did they see in all?

9. Tony ran 15 laps on Monday. He ran 17 laps on Tuesday. How many laps did Tony run altogether?

10. Malcolm found 43 acorns on the ground. Beth found 51 acorns on the ground. How many acorns did they find in all?

© Carson-Dellosa

Read the story. Then, follow the directions below.

Crystal's Backpack

Crystal waved good-bye to her parents and threw her striped backpack over her shoulder. She found her best friend, Sarah, on the bus and sat next to her. "Camp will be so much fun," Sarah said, "but I think I will miss my family."

Crystal unzipped her backpack. "Maybe an apple will help you feel better," she said.

The girls finished their snack in no time. They watched out the window as busy highways became small roads and buildings became lakes. "This makes me feel homesick," Sarah said as she slumped down.

"I have cards in the pocket of my backpack. Should we play?" Crystal asked.

"Okay," answered Sarah. She beat Crystal twice. By the time they started their third game, Sarah had forgotten all about being homesick.

Use details from the story to find which backpack below belongs to Crystal. Circle it. You may want to reread the story, watching for details about the backpack.

FACTOID: The first summer camp was formed in Connecticut in 1861.

© Carson-Dellosa

Look at the 3-D shapes and their names on the chart. Next, count each 3-D shape in the picture. Then, color the boxes in the graph to show how many of each shape you find.

6					
5					
4					
3					
2					
1					
	sphere	cube	cone	rectangular prism	cylinder

© Carson-Dellosa

Subtract to solve each problem. Use the tens blocks for help.

1. 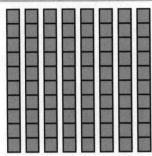   70
                  − 30

2. 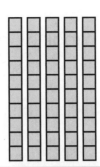   50
                  − 20

3. 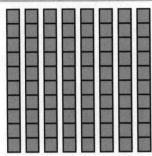   80
                  − 10

4. 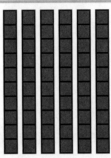   60
                  − 50

Write each word from the box under the word that has the same vowel sound.

bread	leak	steam	deaf
beach	sheep	head	weather

meet   **red**

_____   _____

_____   _____

_____   _____

91

© Carson-Dellosa

Read the passage. Then, follow the directions below.

Pretty Pancakes!

Butterflies are lovely to look at, but here is how to make one you can eat!

Materials:
- 2 frozen pancakes
- 1 banana
- 2 grapes
- 2 sausage links
- jelly or jam
- 2 toothpicks

Directions:
1. Toast two pancakes and cut them in half. Arrange the pieces on a plate to look like the four wings of a butterfly.
2. Peel the banana and place it on the plate. This will be the butterfly's body.
3. Spread jelly or jam on the "wings."
4. Use the toothpicks to hold the grapes like eyes on the banana.
5. Cook the sausage. Then, place it at the top of the banana as antennae.

Use details from the passage to fill in the missing words.

1. The _____ will make the butterfly's body.

2. The wings will be covered with _____ .

3. Butterflies have four _____ .

4. The antennae will be made from _____ .

5. A butterfly has two _____ to see with.

© Carson-Dellosa

Write each word from the box under the word that has the same vowel sound.

boat	drove	box	job
rock	soap	chose	top

home   **cot**

_____

_____

_____

Write the number and its expanded form.

1. 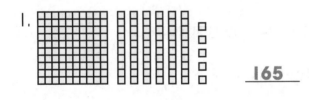 _165_

   _100_ + _60_ + _5_ = _165_

2. 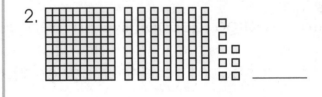 _____

   _____ + _____ + _____ = _____

3. 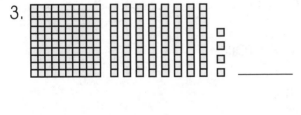 _____

   _____ + _____ + _____ = _____

4. 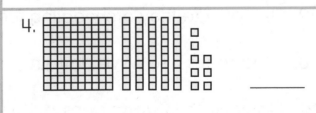 _____

   _____ + _____ + _____ = _____

© Carson-Dellosa

Subtract to find each difference.

1. 49 − 39 10	2. 87 − 6	3. 36 − 24	4. 54 − 40	5. 68 − 16
6. 79 − 63	7. 78 − 25	8. 42 − 12	9. 19 − 7	10. 26 − 11
11. 59 − 38	12. 28 − 14	13. 95 − 62	14. 74 − 50	15. 67 − 41

Read the sentences below. Circle the adjectives.

Example: Kirsten made some (cold,) (sweet) lemonade.

16. A large raccoon lives in the woods near my house.

17. Raccoons have four legs and bushy tails.

18. They have black patches on their faces.

19. It looks like they are wearing funny masks.

20. Raccoons also have dark rings on their tails.

21. They sleep in warm dens in the winter.

22. Raccoons eat fresh fruit, eggs, and insects.

© Carson-Dellosa

Will the figures stack flat on top of each other? Circle yes or no.

1.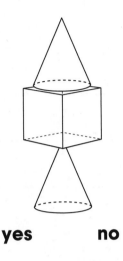

yes   no

2.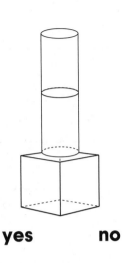

yes   no

3.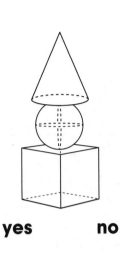

yes   no

Draw a line to divide each compound word into two words. Write the words on the line.

4. fireworks

_____

5. baseball

_____

6. daytime

_____

7. bookcase

_____

8. spaceship

_____

9. railroad

_____

10. eyeball

_____

11. skateboard

_____

 REMINDER: As you research your vacation spot, remember to go to multiple sources for information. Try different websites, reference books, and travel guides.

© Carson-Dellosa

If you could be any animal in the world, what would you be and why? Write a paragraph to explain.

_____

_____

_____

_____

_____

_____

Write the number and the number name.

1.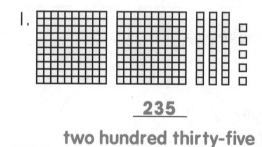

   <u>235</u>

   two hundred thirty-five

2.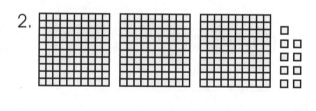

   _____

   _____

3.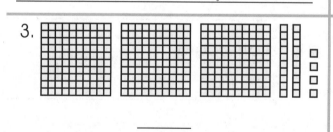

   _____

   _____

4.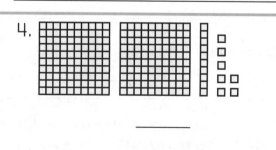

   _____

   _____

© Carson-Dellosa

The Reasons for Rules

All communities have rules. Rules help make things fair and keep people safe. Read the park rules below. Why do you think these rules exist? Write one way each rule might help people. The first one is done for you.

Park Rules

No littering This keeps the park nice for everyone to enjoy.

_____

No dogs _____

_____

No glass containers _____

_____

No loud music _____

_____

No bare feet _____

_____

© Carson-Dellosa

Crystal Rock Candy

Learn about how crystals form with this delicious experiment!

Materials:

- 4 cups sugar
- 1 cup water
- saucepan
- 4 clear, thick glasses or canning jars
- 4 metal spoons
- 4 pencils
- string
- scissors

Procedure:

NOTE: You will need an adult's help. **Do not try this experiment on your own.**

Step One: Measure and cut three pieces of string per glass. The string should be long enough to hang in the solution, just above the bottom of the glass. Add a little extra length so you can tie the string to the pencil.

Step Two: Tie three pieces of string to each pencil—as shown in the picture.

Step Three: Pour one cup of water into a saucepan. Add two cups of sugar. Heat the mixture on the stove, stirring until all the sugar is dissolved. Then, add two more cups of sugar and continue heating and stirring until clear.

Step Four: Place a metal spoon in each glass to help keep it from breaking. Pour the sugar water into the glasses. Add food coloring if you want your crystals to be colored.

Step Five: Set one pencil atop each glass so that the strings hang in the sugar water.

Step Six: In a few hours, check the strings in your glasses. Some crystals should already have formed! Leave the strings in the water until you are happy with the amount of crystals attached. Then, if you'd like, take them out and eat the crystals off the string!

© Carson-Dellosa

Subtract to find each difference.

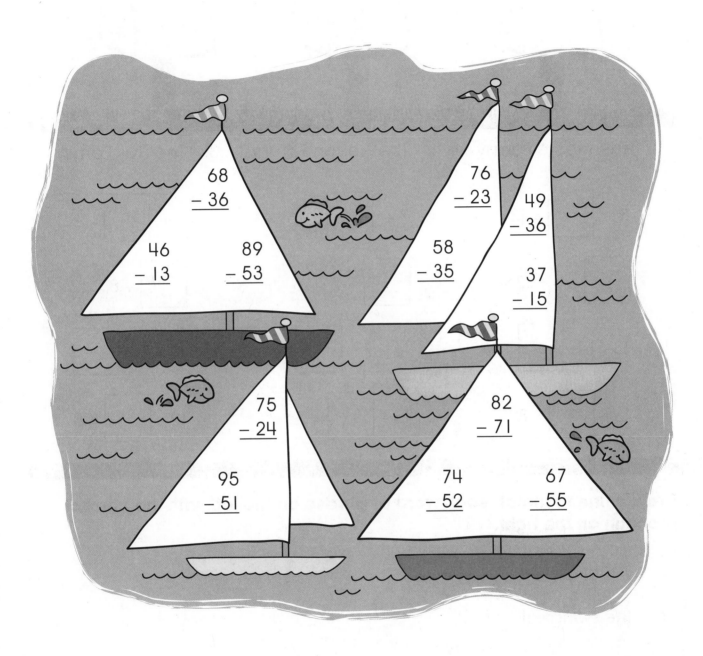

$$68 - 36$$

$$46 - 13$$

$$89 - 53$$

$$76 - 23$$

$$49 - 36$$

$$58 - 35$$

$$37 - 15$$

$$75 - 24$$

$$95 - 51$$

$$82 - 71$$

$$74 - 52$$

$$67 - 55$$

CHARACTER CHECK: Today, when someone says something you don't like, count to 10 and think before saying something back.

© Carson-Dellosa

Use basic addition and subtraction facts to find each family's name. Then, write the name on the correct mailbox.

1. The Moore Family   2. The Nelson Family   3. The Hall Family

8 + ☐ = 13   7 + ☐ = 16   8 + ☐ = 12

☐ + 8 = 13   ☐ + 7 = 16   ☐ + 8 = 12

13 − 8 = ☐   16 − 7 = ☐   12 − 8 = ☐

13 − ☐ = 8   16 − ☐ = 7   12 − ☐ = 8

Draw a line to match each word or phrase on the left with the correct pronoun on the right.

4. Jacob   he

5. the swing set   they

6. Eliza   it

7. Mom and Dad   she

© Carson-Dellosa

Follow the directions below.

1. Write a sentence that describes an animal you have seen in the wild. Use two adjectives.

    _____

    _____

2. Where do you think this animal lives? Write a sentence that describes the animal's home. Use two adjectives.

    _____

    _____

Follow the directions below.

3. Count by 5. Start at 600.

    600, 605, __**610**__ , _____, _____, 625, 630, _____

4. Count by 10. Start at 350.

    350, _____, 370, _____, _____, 400, _____, _____

5. Count by 100. Start at 100.

    100, _____, 300, _____, _____, 600, _____

6. Count backward by 100. Start at 900.

    900, 800, _____, _____, 500, _____, _____

© Carson-Dellosa

Write the numeral for each number word.

1.

one _____

ten _____

six _____

four _____

2.

five _____

zero _____

eleven _____

seven _____

3.

three _____

fourteen _____

thirty _____

sixteen _____

4.

thirty-one _____

thirteen _____

forty-three _____

eighty-nine _____

Be Enthusiastic

Think of something you do not normally enjoy doing. Maybe it's taking out the trash, cleaning your room, or loading the dishwasher. Now, find at least one way to make that activity fun. Can you make a game out of it? What if you sing while you work? Write your ideas on the lines below.

_____

_____

_____

© Carson-Dellosa

Say the name of each picture. Write oa, oo, or ow to complete each word.

1.

s____ ____p

2.

b____ ____t

3.

f____ ____t

4.

p____ ____l

5.

m____n

6.

b____ ____l

Solve each problem.

7. The school play will have 14 tigers, 6 jaguars, and 16 lions. How many wild cats will there be in all?

8. There are 22 boys and 27 girls in the play. How many total children are in the play?

9. Three dads and 16 moms are making costumes. How many parents are helping altogether?

10. The school sold 32 adult tickets and 68 child tickets. How many tickets did they sell combined?

FACTOID: Tigers are the biggest cats on the planet.

© Carson-Dellosa

Write the numeral for each number word.

1. six hundred ninety-six _____
2. twenty-one _____
3. eighty-seven _____
4. ninety-seven _____
5. three hundred sixty-two _____
6. five hundred sixty-one _____
7. seventy-nine _____
8. fifty-four _____
9. twenty-eight _____
10. seven hundred sixty _____
11. one hundred eighteen _____
12. one thousand _____

Make your bedroom sound like the most interesting place on Earth. Describe it in detail, using lots of bold adjectives.

_____

_____

_____

_____

_____

_____

_____

© Carson-Dellosa

Read the story. Circle True if a sentence is true. Circle False if it is false.

Josh and the Bear

Josh heard something outside in the woods. It was still dark. Ma and Pa were sleeping. Josh lit the candle by his bed. There was no window in the little cabin. Josh went to the front door and looked out. Little dark eyes looked back at him. The little dark eyes were part of a big dark face.

Slam! Josh shut the door. He put the big wooden bar across it.

He ran over to the bed and shook his father. "Pa," he said. "Hurry! Bear!" He was too scared to say anything else.

Ma and Pa sat up in bed. Suddenly, they heard a polite knock on the door. Then, the bear began to sing. Josh peeked through the keyhole. He saw the bear juggling four apples. Josh couldn't believe his eyes!

1.	Josh was afraid.	True	False
2.	The thing at the door was a mountain lion.	True	False
3.	Josh closed the door and put a wooden bar across it.	True	False
4.	Josh was awake before Pa.	True	False
5.	This story could have taken place a long time ago.	True	False
6.	The story takes place at noon.	True	False
7.	The story is very likely about a true event.	True	False

REMINDER: Have you been keeping an eye out for interesting animals? Remember to pay attention to what each animal is doing as you observe.

© Carson-Dellosa

Read the sentences below. Write S if the sentence is a statement. Write Q if it is a question. Write E if it is an exclamation. Write C if it is a command.

1. _____ Aidan looked at the treasure map.

2. _____ Walk eleven paces in a straight line from the mailbox.

3. _____ Take six huge steps toward the pond.

4. _____ Aidan found an empty hole.

5. _____ The treasure had disappeared!

6. _____ Who could have taken it?

Write odd or even.

7.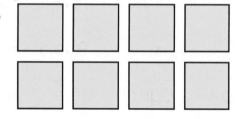

_____

8.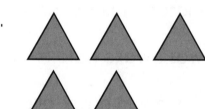

_____

9.

_____

10.

_____

© Carson-Dellosa

Classify your day into three groups: morning, afternoon, and evening.
Write three activities that belong in each group.

My Day

My Morning

1. _____

2. _____

3. _____

My Afternoon

4. _____

5. _____

6. _____

My Evening

7. _____

8. _____

9. _____

© Carson-Dellosa

Color the shape with the number that matches the description.

1. 293 292

two hundreds, nine tens, and three ones

2. 955 995

nine hundreds, nine tens, and five ones

3. 230 323

two hundreds, 3 tens, and zero ones

4. 100 200

one hundred, zero tens, and zero ones

5. 260 320

three hundreds, two tens, and zero ones

6. 517 570

five hundreds, one ten, and 7 ones

Use the subjects and verbs to write compound sentences. Add other words as needed. Make sure to put a comma before each conjunction.

Subjects	
the baby	the girl
the bus	your dad
the car	your mom

Verbs	
cleaned	hopped
cooked	stopped
crawled	walked

Example: The baby crawled, and the girl walked.

7. _____

8. _____

9. _____

© Carson-Dellosa

Recycling Challenge

Collecting recycling is a great way to be a good citizen. Recycling used paper and containers means that these materials don't have to be made again from scratch. That saves energy! Recycling also keeps trash from traveling to faraway landfills, which means less air pollution from trucks and trains.

See how many recyclables you can collect in a week. Keep track of the number of paper, plastic, glass, and metal items. Make sure you rinse out any food or drink containers, and stay away from glass and metal containers with sharp or jagged edges. Finally, don't forget to either place your bin outside on recycling day or take it with an adult to a recycling center.

Put a tally mark in the appropriate column for every item you collect.

Paper	Plastic	Metal	Glass

© Carson-Dellosa

Listen and Learn
(for two or more players)

This game will help you practice both your listening skills and your teaching skills. See how well you give and follow directions!

How to Play:

All players write down detailed instructions for something they know how to do well. This should be an activity that can be completed in two minutes or less. For example, someone might write directions for drawing a cartoon character, for throwing a spiral football pass, or even for pantomiming driving a bus. Players should make sure that they have any supplies they need for their activity.

When everyone is ready, players take turns reading their directions out loud while everyone else follows those directions.

Director's Job: Without telling the listeners what the activity is, the director slowly and clearly reads the directions, making sure there is time for the listeners to follow each step. The director should not repeat any of the steps.

Actors' Job: The actors listen carefully and follow the directions exactly. No steps should be repeated, so players must listen the first time around!

The goal of this game is for the actors to learn what the director teaches. Were the actors able to follow the directions? Did what they do match what the director was thinking?

Alternate Play:

The first player to know what activity is being taught can choose to drop out of the game and whisper his or her guess to the reader. If the guess is correct, that player gets a point, but if it's incorrect, that player loses a point. You may need to ask an adult to be the judge in this version of the game.

© Carson-Dellosa

Trip Planner, Step 3

If you're like most people, you want to know what the food is like where you're going. See what you can find out about what people eat in your vacation spot. Is the place known for any specific food?

For example, Philadelphia is know for its Philly cheese steaks, and Paris is known for its croissants. Find out what you should eat to get the full experience of the place you're visiting. Ask your family to help you find out what food the place is known for. Then, see if you can find some pictures of that food. If you're feeling really adventurous, ask an adult to help you cook something from that region!

List the foods you can expect to eat while on vacation. Be sure to include anything the place is specifically known for.

_____

_____

_____

_____

_____

_____

_____

_____

© Carson-Dellosa

Adopt an Animal, Step 2

Now that you have a list of animals in the wild, choose the animal that you would most like to adopt. Think about these questions before you make your final decision:

- Which animal would be the easiest to take care of?
- Which would be the hardest to take care of?
- Which animal would be the most fun to play with?
- Where in the house would your new pet live?

Choose your favorite animal from your list, and draw it in your house.

© Carson-Dellosa

Adopt an Animal, Step 3

You want to be sure that your new pet will be happy and healthy. To do that, you'll need to find out everything you can about the animal you want to adopt. Find books at the library, or search the Internet for information on your chosen animal. Ask an adult for help finding websites with useful information.

NOTE: Since many wild animals are not recommended as pets, you may have to take your best guess about how to care for your chosen animal. Just base your guess on the information you find about how that animal lives.

Answer the questions below to prepare for bringing home your imaginary pet.

1. What food does it eat? _____

2. Does it sleep during the day or night? _____

3. How much space does it need to be comfortable? _____

   _____

4. How active is this animal? How does it get exercise? _____

   _____

5. Does it like to cuddle or have contact with other animals? Explain.

   _____

6. What is the biggest danger for this animal in your house? How will you keep your new pet safe?

   _____

© Carson-Dellosa

Write i or e to show what sound the y makes in each word.

1. _____ cry

2. _____ pony

3. _____ penny

4. _____ twenty

5. _____ try

6. _____ city

7. _____ baby

8. _____ lady

9. _____ fly

10. _____ bunny

11. _____ fry

12. _____ jelly

Write how long each object is in inches.

13.

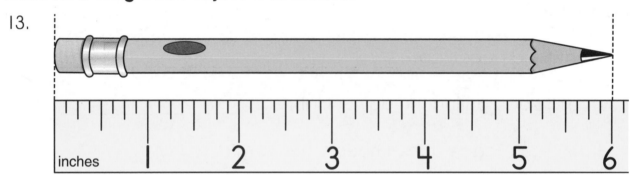

_____ inches

14.

15.

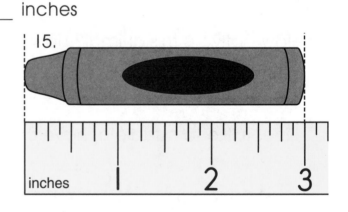

_____ inches

_____ inches

CHARACTER CHECK: You can be kind even when you disagree with someone. What are some kind ways to say you don't agree?

© Carson-Dellosa

Read the story. Then, follow the directions below.

A Great Castle!

Jessica and Alex are building a castle. Jessica builds the walls with brown wooden squares. Alex adds the green triangle roof. Jessica balances the long yellow cylinder towers. Alex tops them with red cones. Jessica puts blue rectangles inside for beds. Alex builds a path with small orange cubes. At last they are finished. That is great teamwork!

Mark an X in each box to show which child used each shape.

Shapes	Jessica	Alex
triangles		
rectangles		
squares		
cylinders		
cubes		
cones		

Draw the castle.

© Carson-Dellosa

Use context clues to make the best choice for each bold word's meaning. Circle your choice.

1. The blue paint turned a **pale** color when I added water to it.

    bright   light   bucket

2. My brother found a **blade** of grass on his shoe.

    piece   knife   wheel

3. Dad likes to relax on the **sofa** after he takes us swimming.

    bike   couch   stairs

4. Would you like a large or small **portion** of watermelon?

    drink   slice   picnic

5. Prairie dogs sit on **mounds** to help them see danger coming.

    their tails   small hills   mountains

6. The aquarium has many **rare** fish that would be hard to see anywhere else.

    special   slightly cooked   scary

7. The cowboy tried to **calm** the neighing horses after the loud thunder ended.

    quiet   move   anger

FACTOID: Prairie dogs are not dogs at all—they are members of the squirrel family!

© Carson-Dellosa

Use the ruler to measure each line to the nearest centimeter. Then, write each length.

I centimeter (cm)

1. _____ = _____ centimeters

2. _____ = _____ centimeters

3. _____ = _____ centimeters

4. _____ = _____ centimeters

5. _____ = _____ centimeters

Use a ruler to measure the sides of each shape to the nearest centimeter. Then, add.

6. _____ + _____ + _____ + _____ = _____ cm

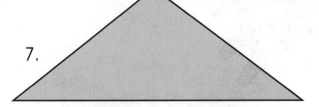

7. _____ + _____ + _____ = _____ cm

8. _____ + _____ + _____ + _____ = _____ cm

© Carson-Dellosa

Use context clues in each description to help you choose the meaning of the bold word. Circle your choice.

1. It was a **pleasant** day. The sky was blue and the sun was warm. We put on our swimsuits. We ran down to the beach.

    dull   nice   sad

2. It was hot outside. Toby went to gather some eggs. All of the hens were asleep **beneath** the porch.

    under   above   with

3. Irma fell down in the yard during lunch. She hurt her arm. The **ache** got worse when she carried a big box for Mrs. Wilson.

    dream   page   pain

4. Some dinosaurs were small, but brachiosaurs were **huge**.

    fast   big   old

Use a ruler to measure each object to the nearest centimeter.

5.   _____ cm

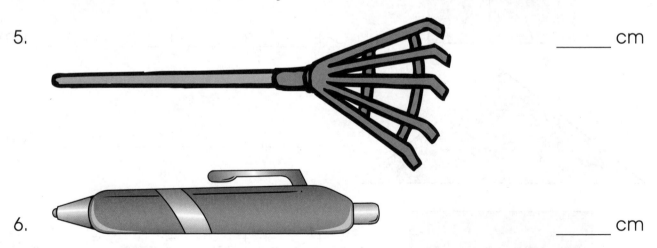

6.   _____ cm

© Carson-Dellosa

Describe the perfect vacation spot. Help the reader to see, hear, smell, taste, and feel what it's like to be there.

_____

_____

_____

_____

_____

_____

Write the correct punctuation mark at the end of each sentence. Use (.), (!), or (?).

1. Are we going to the game_____

2. Look out for the ball_____

3. You are so amazing_____

4. Are reindeer real animals_____

5. The girl on the swing is my sister_____

FITNESS FLASH: March around the house or yard for 2 minutes. Try singing to the rhythm of your feet!

© Carson-Dellosa

Read the passage.

Germs

Germs are things you should not share. Germs can make you sick. Even though you cannot see germs, they get into the body in many ways. Germs get in the body through the nose, mouth, eyes, and cuts in the skin. We share germs when we sneeze or cough and do not cover our mouths. We share germs when we drink from the same cup or eat from the same plate.

To keep germs to yourself and to get well:

- Wash your hands with soap.
- Cover your mouth when you cough or sneeze.
- Do not share food or drink.
- Keep your fingers away from your nose, mouth, and eyes.
- Drink lots of water.
- Get lots of fresh air.
- Eat healthy meals.
- Get plenty of sleep.

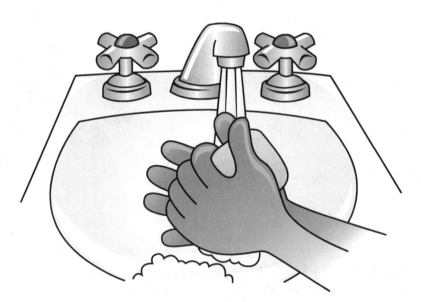

© Carson-Dellosa

Answer the questions about the passage on page 120.

1. What is the main idea?
   A. Germs are things you do not want to share.
   B. You can't see germs.
   C. Wash your hands often.

2. Put an **X** next to the ways you can keep germs to yourself.

   _____ Wash your hands with soap.

   _____ Stay away from animals.

   _____ Cover your mouth when you cough or sneeze.

   _____ Get plenty of sleep.

   _____ Eat healthy meals.

3. Put a **T** next to the sentences that are true. Put an **F** next to the sentences that are false.

   _____ Germs can make you sick.

   _____ Germs cannot get in your body through the nose, mouth, eyes, and cuts in the skin.

   _____ Cover your mouth when you cough or sneeze to keep germs to yourself.

Circle the correct short vowel.

4. Germs can make you s ___ ck.

   i   o

5. Germs get in the body through c ___ ts in the skin.

   a   u

6. Cover your mo ___ th when you cough.

   o   u

7. Get l ___ ts of fresh air.

   i   o

Use the dictionary entry below to answer the questions.

germ (jûrm), n. 1. a disease-producing microbe. 2. a bud or seed.

8. What part of speech is *germ*?

   _____

9. Use the word **germ** in a sentence.

   _____

   _____

   _____

© Carson-Dellosa

Complete each table.

1.

Subtract 6	
9	3
6	
11	
10	
12	
8	

2.

Subtract 4	
7	
9	
10	
8	
6	
13	

3.

Subtract 5	
11	
7	
14	
5	
8	
12	

Say the name of each picture. Write the vowels to complete each word.

4.

s_____ _____l

5.

_____ _____nk

6.

c_____ _____n

CHARACTER CHECK: Practice determination. Take an extra long walk with an adult. When you get tired, press on until you reach your goal.

© Carson-Dellosa

Time To Go Home

This map shows routes the dinosaur can take to get to its cave. Use the key to find each symbol on the map. Then, follow the directions.

Dinosaur Cave Map

Directions:

1. Write the word **H O M E** on the dinosaur cave.

2. Color the volcano on the map red.

3. Color the trees on the map green.

4. Draw a blue line to show a route the dinosaur can take home that goes past the volcano.

5. Draw a yellow line to show another route the dinosaur can take home. Make the route go past the rocks.

© Carson-Dellosa

BONUS

Take It Outside!

Go outside and see if you can find exactly 100 of the same natural object. For example, you might find 100 pinecones, 100 small rocks, or 100 acorns. Count your natural objects by putting them into groups of ten.

Bring a sheet of drawing paper and some crayons outside. Choose a spot with some trees and plants. Fold your paper in half. On one side of the fold, draw the spot how it looks now. On the other side of the fold, draw how you think the spot will look during the winter.

Fill a tub or wading pool with water outside. Get several objects that will not be harmed if they get wet. Stand up tall and drop each object into the water. Listen for the sound each object makes. What makes the loudest sounding splash, and what makes the softest? Which ones float and which ones sink? Do you notice any similarities between the objects that make a loud splash? What do the objects that sink have in common?

© Carson-Dellosa

Write the time shown on each clock.

1.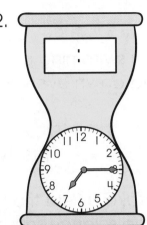

2.

3.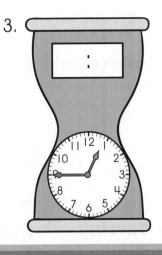

4.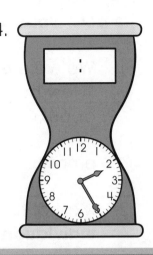

Use a ruler to measure each item to the nearest centimeter. Then, answer the questions.

5.

How long is the log? _____

How long is the saw? _____

How much longer is the log than the saw? _____

6.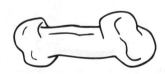

How long is the bone? _____

How long is the dog? _____

How much longer is the dog than the bone? _____

© Carson-Dellosa

Use context clues in each sentence to help you choose the meaning of the bold word. Circle your choice.

1. We were **ecstatic** about the new swimming pool. We cheered, "New pool!" and jumped up and down every time we thought about it.

    empty   happy   pretty

2. Most of the students wanted to take a field trip to the zoo, but some **individuals** would rather go to the science museum.

    people   animals   buses

3. The weather report said there would be no chance of **precipitation** today, but it stormed all afternoon anyway.

    rain or snow   leaving for a trip   a bad day

Circle the correct rule for each number pattern.

4.

6, 8, 10, 12, 14, 16

+1   +2

5.

20, 18, 16, 14, 12, 10

−2   −3

6.

30, 40, 50, 60, 70, 80

−10   +10

7.

80, 79, 78, 77, 76, 75

+10   −1

© Carson-Dellosa

Write the time shown on each clock.

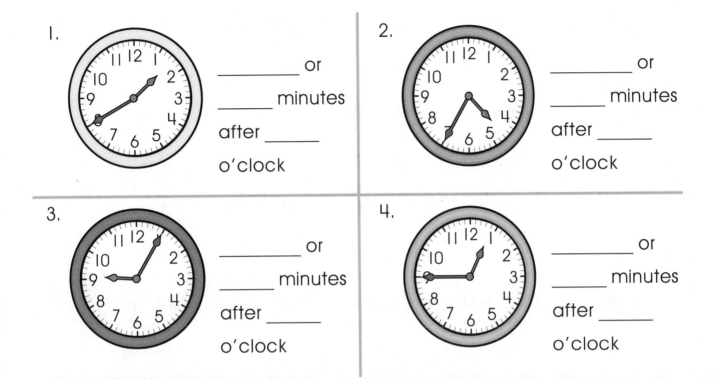

1. _____ or
   _____ minutes
   after _____
   o'clock

2. _____ or
   _____ minutes
   after _____
   o'clock

3. _____ or
   _____ minutes
   after _____
   o'clock

4. _____ or
   _____ minutes
   after _____
   o'clock

Reading Hopscotch

Using sidewalk chalk, set up a hopscotch course with 10 boxes. In each box, write a word you know from first grade. Make sure you spell it correctly. To play, toss a small stone into one of the boxes. That's the box you will need to stop in to pick up your stone. As you hop in each box, read the word as you hit the ground. If you jump on a double box, read both words.

also give walk think

nice many boy

© Carson-Dellosa

Circle the word in each row that does not belong.

1. scissors   carrot   books   paper   pencils

2. train   jet   leg   car   boat

3. cat   dog   green   fish   bird

4. lake   ocean   pond   chair   river

5. bear   apple   orange   peach   plum

6. Jane   Kathy   Tom   Jill   Ann

7. park   scared   library   school   home

8. tulip   daffodil   rose   daisy   basket

Use the unfinished sentence below to start a story. Use your imagination and be as descriptive as possible.

Under the stairs in a small green basket is . . .

_____

_____

_____

_____

_____

© Carson-Dellosa

Draw the hands on each clock to show the time. Circle a.m. or p.m.

1. four o'clock in the morning

a.m.

p.m.

2. seven thirty in the evening

a.m.

p.m.

3. eleven forty-five at night

a.m.

p.m.

4. ten fifteen in the morning

a.m.

p.m.

Count the coins in each problem. Write how much money is shown.

5.

____ + ____ + ____ + ____ = ____ ¢

6.

____ + ____ + ____ = ____ ¢

7.

____ + ____ + ____ + ____ = ____ ¢

8.

____ + ____ + ____ + ____ = ____ ¢

© Carson-Dellosa

Read the story.

Abby

My dog, Abby, loves to go to the river. Every Saturday morning, I take Abby to the park by the river to play. The first thing Abby does when we get there is run down to the water.

Abby likes to splash in the water. The cold water doesn't bother her. When she gets out of the water, she shakes and shakes. I stand back so that the water does not get on me. Then, she looks for a rock in the sun to take a nap on. She sleeps there until I whistle for her when it is time to go home.

I think our Saturday trips to the river are something that Abby looks forward to all week.

© Carson-Dellosa

Answer the questions about the story on page 130.

1. What is the main idea?
   A. Abby takes a nap.
   B. Abby loves trips to the river.
   C. Abby is a good dog.

2. Number the events in the order that they happened in the story.

   _____ I whistle for Abby when it is time to go home.

   _____ Abby runs to the water.

   _____ Abby takes a nap.

   _____ Abby splashes in the water.

3. What does Abby do when she gets out of the water?
   A. rolls in the dirt
   B. shakes and shakes
   C. licks her fur

Circle the correct short vowel.

4. I have a d ___ g.

   i   o

5. Abby likes to spl ___ sh in the water.

   a   i

6. Abby n ___ ps on a rock.

   i   a

7. Abby finds a rock in the s ___ n.

   u   a

Sometimes the same word can be used as a noun or as a verb. Write noun or verb to tell how the bold word is used in each sentence.

8. Can I have a **drink**, please?

   _____

9. My dogs **drink** a lot of water.

   _____

10. My dog made a big **splash** in the water.

    _____

11. The children **splash** in the water.

    _____

12. I order a **shake** with my burger.

    _____

13. My hands **shake** when I am nervous.

    _____

© Carson-Dellosa

Write the correct word to complete each sentence.

1. A quarter is a _____ .

   coin   coyn

2. I hope the new baby is a _____ .

   boi   boy

3. The tiger showed its _____ .

   claws   claus

4. Dan has two sons and one _____ .

   daughter   dawter

Solve each problem.

$7 $3 $12 $26

5. Coral bought a watch and a book. How much money did she spend?

6. Jamey bought a baseball and a toothbrush. How much money did he spend?

7. Maria bought a baseball and a watch. How much money did she spend?

8. Alejandro bought a toothbrush and a book. How much money did he spend?

© Carson-Dellosa

Which sport is the most popular with your friends and family? Ask each person to choose a favorite sport from the list. Make a tally mark beside each answer given. Then, color the boxes to graph your results.

volleyball _____

football _____

soccer _____

baseball _____

basketball _____

other _____

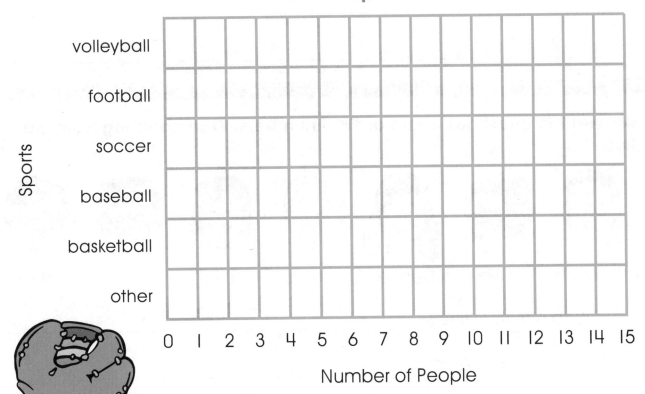

Favorite Sports

FACTOID: The average volleyball player jumps up to 300 times in one match!

© Carson-Dellosa

Use the sentence below to start a story. Use your imagination and be as descriptive as possible.

When you turn eight years old, something very interesting happens.

_____

_____

_____

_____

_____

Answer the questions about ordinal numbers. Start counting from the left.

Grayson   Allie   Denise   Tanner   Lori   Matt   Rob

1. Who is third in line? _____.

2. Who is sixth in line? _____.

3. Who is seventh in line? _____.

4. Who is second in line? _____.

5. Who is fourth in line? _____.

© Carson-Dellosa

Trip Planner, Final Step

You have researched your vacation spot in detail. Now, show others what's so great about this place! Follow the directions below and the example on the next page to create your own travel brochure.

Materials:
- a sheet of $8\frac{1}{2}$ " x 11" plain white paper
- pictures of your vacation spot attractions
- attractions, weather, and food information
- markers or colored pencils
- pencil or pen

Directions:
1. Place an $8\frac{1}{2}$ " x 11" sheet of paper longwise on a table. Fold it into three equal sections. Start by folding the right side over and then the left. You are now looking at the front of your brochure, which should open from right to left.

2. On the front, include the place name (use a catchy title if you like) and a picture of the place.

3. On the back of the brochure, write a sentence that sums up the place. This is also where you can write your name as the designer and author.

4. Open your brochure all the way. Use the left and middle panels (pages 2 and 3 of the brochure) for your attractions. Include your pictures and information from page 73.

5. Next, use the right panel for the food you want to feature. Include your pictures and food descriptions from page 111.

6. Finally, flip your brochure over and use the remaining panel (page 5) for your weather information. Include weather and packing advice from page 87.

© Carson-Dellosa

Trip Planner
Finished Product Example
How to Fold your Brochure

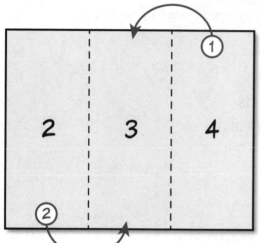

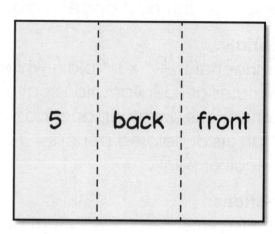

Sample Brochure Pages

2   3   4

Under each attraction picture, the author included one sentence about the place in the picture.

The pictures of food speak for themselves!

front

The front cover has a picture of a famous attraction.

back

This author chose to include a picture of himself on the back cover.

© Carson-Dellosa

Adopt an Animal, Final Step

Use the information you recorded on page 113 to put together an "adoption request." Show that you have thought of everything your adopted pet will need to be healthy and happy. For each of your pet's needs, draw a picture to illustrate exactly how that need will be met at your house. Be sure to include a picture of you and your pet playing together as well.

On a separate sheet of paper, sketch out your ideas. Then, follow the directions below and the examples on the next page to put together your proposal.

Materials:
- construction paper
- plain white paper
- markers, crayons, and/or colored pencils
- pencil or pen
- glue
- stapler

Directions:

1. Name your pet. You can use this name throughout your proposal.

2. Use a separate sheet of plain white paper for each of your pet's needs. Draw and color a picture of how each of your pet's needs will be met at your house. Then, write a sentence to explain (for example, "Bertha will be fed red meat once a day").

3. Make a cover for your proposal. On plain white paper, draw a picture of you and your pet playing together to put on the cover. Then, give your proposal a title like "Adoption Request" or "How I Will Care for my Pet."

4. Glue each drawing to a sheet of construction paper.

5. Put your pictures in order. Think about which order works best for making a strong case. You might want to have the most emotional picture at the end of the proposal.

6. Staple the pages together to make a book.

© Carson-Dellosa

Adopt an Animal
Finished Product Example

Have fun designing your adoption request! Here are examples of each page, including the cover:

Taking care of my raccoon.

Rocky will live in the house with me and my family.

Rocky will have his own room with his own bed.

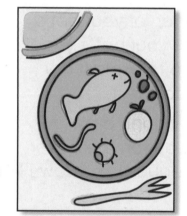

Rocky will eat lots of different foods to stay healthy.

Rocky will get exercise by running and playing whenever he wants.

Rocky will be LOVED.

© Carson-Dellosa

Anchors Away

Solve the addition problems. Use the code to find the answer to this riddle:

What did the pirate have to do before every trip out to sea?

48	36	58	96	69	75	89	29
O	H	G	B	T	E	N	A

EXAMPLE:

42 +16	34 +41	60 + 9
58		
G		

17 +31	55 +34

26 +43	14 + 22	52 + 23

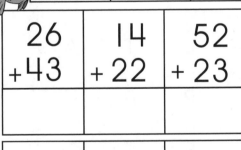

83 +13	24 +24	5 +24	52 +17
			!

© Carson-Dellosa

BONUS

Space Words

Find and circle the space words in the puzzle below. The words go across and down. Use the word bank to help you.

Moon	Shuttle	Land	Orbit
Flight	Comet	Astronaut	Star
Rocket	Planet	Space	Sun

```
S  S  S  O  R  B  I  T  M  A
G  U  R  L  A  N  D  C  S
W  N  R  A  F  P  L  O  T
S  H  U  T  T  L  E  M  R
T  X  N  S  P  A  C  E  O
A  F  M  O  O  N  T  T  N
R  V  E  B  A  E  U  T  A
F  L  I  G  H  T  P  R  U
L  F  R  O  C  K  E  T  T
```

© Carson-Dellosa

Section III Introduction

Theme: My Summer Adventures

This month's explorations invite your child to reflect on her experiences as the end of summer vacation approaches. They encourage her to use her growing skills to tell her own stories in imaginative ways. Before the beginning of a new school year, take the time to talk with your child about how much she has grown and changed. Measure and record her height and weight and look back at old photos together. Ask her to show off how good she is at swimming, playing sports, reading and writing sentences, doing math problems, and other skills that show her growing maturity. Make sure to ask what she is looking forward to learning in the new school year.

To build language arts and literacy skills this month, visit the library and challenge your child to choose a book that is a little longer or more difficult than what she is used to. Read the book to her several times and then ask her to read it to you. Take advantage of back-to-school sales and purchase supplies for a home writing center. These can include pencils, pens, markers, envelopes, notebooks, index cards, and stickers. Encourage your child to write letters and stories for fun every day.

To build math skills this month, challenge your child to notice groups of different objects and add them up for an overall total. Go on a search for two- and three-digit numbers around your home and ask your child to tell you how many hundreds, tens, and ones are in each. Provide a ruler and ask her to measure toys, household items, and even family members. Which object is tallest or longest? Who is the tallest person in the house? How much taller is that person than she is?

Explorations

This month, your child will have a choice of two explorations. He may choose to follow steps for one or both. Review the explorations below with your child and help him make a choice. Emphasize that it is useful to have a path in mind from the start. Then, help your child find and complete the project activities according to his plan. Throughout the section, your child will see the icons shown below on pages that include directions directly related to one of the explorations. Emphasize that breaking a large project into smaller steps helps make it fun and easy to do.

 **Summertime Song**

With this exploration, your child will develop language arts and fine arts skills by making an instrument and writing and performing a song about his summer adventures. Your child will use household items to build and decorate a simple drum. Then, he will think about favorite summer experiences and use them to write verses and a chorus. Finally, he will perform his song for family and friends.

© Carson-Dellosa

Speaking, listening, and performance skills are important to school and personal success. Praise your child's growing ability to speak clearly and confidently. Have fun together using silly poems and tongue twisters to develop speaking skills. As your child rehearses his song, model being a good listener. Encourage him to sing or chant loudly and clearly during the performance. When show time arrives, make a video recording of the event. Watch the video together and congratulate your child on his success.

 **Summer Adventures Picture Book**

With this exploration, your child will develop language arts and writing skills by creating a picture book that chronicles her summer experiences. She will think about adventures such as playing flashlight tag, going to the zoo, or riding her bike. For each experience, she will write a description and take or draw pictures of the beginning, middle, and end of the event. Then, she will write about the three experiences that feel the most like stories. Finally, she will compile her stories into a picture book to share.

To help your child complete this exploration, read simple picture books together and have your child talk about the beginning, middle, and end of each story. Share thoughts about why stories need these three main parts, pointing out the kinds of events that tend to happen in the beginning, middle, and end.

Learning Activities

Practice pages for this month introduce skills your child will learn in the first grade. They also focus on skills that support the explorations described above. Preview the activities and choose several that target skills your child needs to practice. Also select several relating to the exploration(s) your child plans to complete. You may wish to mark those pages with a star or other symbol to let your child know to begin with those. Then, let your child choose practice activities that interest her and allow her to demonstrate her growing skills.

© Carson-Dellosa

Summertime Song, Step 1

Before going back to school, relive the summer! In this exploration, you will turn your favorite summer adventures into an original song!

To begin, think about all the fun things you have done this summer. Did you travel anywhere? Did you have a particularly fun day at the park? Did you sleep over at a friend's house? Make a list of your adventures. Is there anything else you would like to do before back-to-school? Put those on the list, too, and see if you can make them happen. Continue on a separate sheet of paper, if needed.

Summer Adventures

1. _____
2. _____
3. _____
4. _____
5. _____
6. _____
7. _____
8. _____
9. _____
10. _____

© Carson-Dellosa

Summer Adventures Picture Book, Step 1

Use the fun things you do this summer to make a book about you! In this exploration, you will take or draw pictures of your summer adventures. Then, you will turn your favorite adventures into a picture book!

To begin, make a list of your favorite things to do in the summer. Maybe you like having picnics in the park, riding your bike in the neighborhood, or playing flashlight tag with friends. Include any favorite things you have done so far plus anything you would like to do before you go back to school. Continue on a separate sheet of paper, if needed.

Favorite Summer Activities

1. _____

2. _____

3. _____

4. _____

5. _____

6. _____

7. _____

8. _____

9. _____

10. _____

© Carson-Dellosa

Solve each problem.

1. The toy store sold 7  in March,

   3 🤖 in April, and 8 🤖 in May.

   How many 🤖 did the toy store sell in all? _____

---

2. Felicia puts 2 🎎 , 2 🧸 ,

   and 8 🐕 on shelves.

   How many toys does Felicia put on shelves? _____

---

3. The toy store has 8 🚗 , 2 🚚 ,

   and 10 🚜 .

   How many of these toys does the toy store have in all? _____

Active Listening

Practice listening by playing a game of *Red Light, Green Light* with friends. First, decide as a group what kind of movement each color should stand for. For example, *green* means "run" and *yellow* means "crawl." Listen to each other's ideas and come to an agreement. As you play, listen carefully to the leader to know which way to move.

© Carson-Dellosa

Read each statement. Write Y for yes or N for no beside each statement.

How a Snail Is Like a Turtle

1. _____ Both have shells.

2. _____ Both can be on land.

3. _____ Both are reptiles.

4. _____ Both are slimy.

How a Tree Is Like a Flower

5. _____ Both are plants.

6. _____ Both need sunlight.

7. _____ Both have branches.

8. _____ Both need water.

Write a number on each line to tell how many parts of the shape are colored.

9.

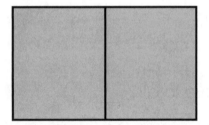

_____ halves

10.

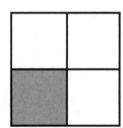

_____ fourth

11.

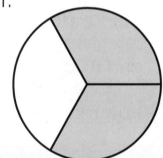

_____ thirds

FACTOID: Escargot is a French dish made of cooked snails.

© Carson-Dellosa

Add to find each sum.

1. 8
    3
    5
    + 2

2. 2
    6
    4
    + 3

3. 1
    9
    2
    + 2

4. 6
    5
    1
    + 2

5. 2
    4
    3
    + 4

6. 9
    2
    3
    + 5

7. 3
    4
    5
    + 3

8. 5
    7
    2
    + 1

9. 6
    1
    8
    + 1

10. 0
     6
     1
     + 4

11. 4
     2
     3
     + 2

12. 7
     8
     2
     + 3

The vowel pair ew can make the long u sound. Write the word from the box that names each picture.

| news | stew | jewelry | screw |

13.  _____

14. _____

15. _____

16. _____

© Carson-Dellosa

Some nouns name groups of people, animals, or things. Choose a noun from the box to complete each sentence.

| class | family | school | herd |

1. My _____ lives at 123 Maple Street.

2. We saw a _____ of cattle grazing in the field.

3. A _____ of fish swam under the dock.

4. On Wednesday, our _____ will take a field trip.

Follow the directions to color the shapes.

5.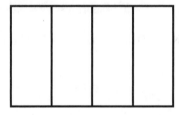

Color three fourths.

6.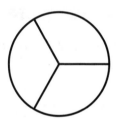

Color one third.

7.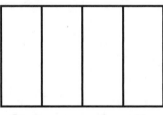

Color one fourth.

8.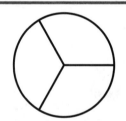

Color two thirds.

CHARACTER CHECK: Write a story about your life. What important events have you experienced? What are your strongest memories?

© Carson-Dellosa

Write the time shown on each clock.

1.

_____

2.

_____

3.

_____

4.

_____

5.

_____

6.

_____

Write two sentences. Use one word from the box in each sentence.

flew	new	few	grew

7. _____

_____

8. _____

_____

© Carson-Dellosa

Count the hundreds, tens, and ones. Write the number.

1.

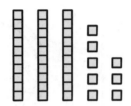

_____ hundreds, _____ tens,

and _____ ones = _____

2.

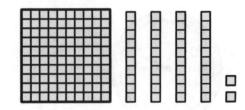

_____ hundred, _____ tens,

and _____ ones = _____

3.

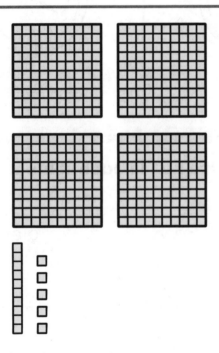

_____ hundreds, _____ ten,

and _____ ones = _____

4.

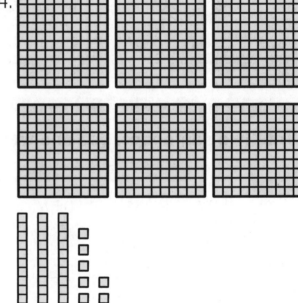

_____ hundreds, _____ tens,

and _____ ones = _____

© Carson-Dellosa

Summer Adventures Picture Book, Step 2

Keep track of the fun things you do this month! Each time you do one of your favorite things, take a picture or draw something to represent your adventure. If possible, include a picture for the beginning, middle, and end of the event. Then, on this sheet, write a brief description of what you did. Continue on a separate sheet of paper. Also, if you would like, check items off your list of favorites on page 144 as you go.

1.	
2.	
3.	
4.	
5.	
6.	
7.	
8.	
9.	
10.	

© Carson-Dellosa

Write the time shown on each clock.

1.

_____

2.

_____

3.

_____

4.

_____

5.

_____

6.

_____

Look up the words in a dictionary. In each pair, circle the word that is misspelled. Write the word correctly on the line.

7. early   thougt   _____

8. caterpilar   scared   _____

9. sents   picnic   _____

10. because   dragin   _____

11. chane   while   _____

12. speshal   coat   _____

FITNESS FLASH: Do 10 sit-ups. See if you can make each one last 5 seconds.

© Carson-Dellosa

In each sentence below, circle the common nouns. Underline the proper nouns.

1. Tasha and Sabrina live on Glenwood Avenue.

2. Once, they had a colony of bats in the attic.

3. Their neighbors Nate, Bryan, and Nikki live in the gray house across the street.

4. They used to live in Michigan before they moved to Maryland.

5. Nate, Nikki, Sabrina, and Tasha take the bus to Bellevue Elementary School.

Use a ruler to measure each object to the nearest inch.

6.

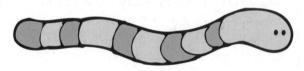

= _____ inches

7.

= _____ inches

8.

= _____ inches

© Carson-Dellosa

Use the calendars to answer each question.

April						
S	M	T	W	Th	F	S
			1	2	3	4
5	6	7	8	9	10	11
12	13	14	15	16	17	18
19	20	21	22	23	24	25
26	27	28	29	30		

May						
S	M	T	W	Th	F	S
					1	2
3	4	5	6	7	8	9
10	11	12	13	14	15	16
17	18	19	20	21	22	23
24	25	26	27	28	29	30
31						

1. Karina went to the dentist on the third Tuesday in April. What was the date?

    Tuesday, April _____

2. Heath started his dance class on the first Monday in June. What was the date?

    Monday, June _____

3. Today is April 10. Adam's family will see a play next Friday. On what date will they see a play?

    Friday, April _____

4. How many days away is May 5 from April 29?

    _____

What is the most exciting part about going back to school?

_____

_____

_____

_____

© Carson-Dellosa

A Walk Around Town

Let's take a walk around the town of Forest Grove. Use a marker or crayon to trace your route.

Directions:

1. Begin your walking tour at Forest Grove Inn.

2. Walk two blocks east to Elm Street.

3. Turn north on Elm Street. Walk to the Museum.

4. Go one-half block north to the corner of Elm and Lincoln.

5. Turn east on Lincoln. Walk until you come to the City Library.

6. Go south on Oak Street until you reach Washington Street.

7. Turn west on Washington and walk two and one-half blocks to the Burger Barn.

8. Lunch is over. Take the shortest way back to Forest Grove Inn.

© Carson-Dellosa

BONUS

See the Light

The pupil plays an important role in eyesight—it is the opening in the eye, which lets in light. That light is then turned into images and sent through the optic nerve to the brain. If there is too much or too little light, the pictures in your brain will not turn out right. So, to stay in control over how much light gets in, your pupils get larger or smaller. Try this experiment to watch your pupils at work!

1. Turn off or dim any bright lights and look into a mirror. Draw your eyes, paying special attention to the size of your pupils.

2. Now, look at a light in the room for a count of 100. Then, draw your eyes again.

3. How did your pupils change from the first to the second step?

First Step	Second Step

© Carson-Dellosa

The vowel pairs ou and ow can make the sound you hear in the middle of mouth and clown. Write the word from the box that names each picture.

| cow | blouse | flower | clown | frown | gown |

1. _____

2. _____

3. _____

4. _____

5. _____

6. _____

Solve each problem. Use the number line to help you add hundreds.

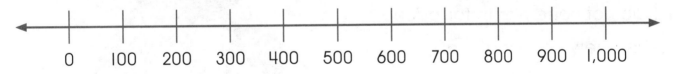

0   100   200   300   400   500   600   700   800   900   1,000

7. 200 + 200 = _____

8. 700 + 300 = _____

9. 100 + 300 = _____

10. 600 + 200 = _____

11. 400 + 400 = _____

12. 500 + 400 = _____

FACTOID: Cows are red-green colorblind.

© Carson-Dellosa

Read the poem.

Teddy

Mom and Dad think I'm too old

to still have my teddy bear.

They say, "You are eight years old now,

and Teddy shows too much wear."

I nod my head and then agree.

I know I'm a real strong kid.

Without a thought I put him up,

and in my closet he hid.

That same night, I tried and tried,

but could not fall asleep.

A storm came in with lots of noise.

I did not make a peep.

Instead, I took my bear out

of the hiding place I made.

I did not need him to fall asleep.

I just knew he was afraid.

© Carson-Dellosa

Answer the questions about the poem on page 158.

1. Why do the parents want the child to put the teddy bear away?

    A. They think that the child is too old to have a teddy bear.

    B. They think that the child will lose the bear.

    C. They want the child to play with other toys.

    D. They think that teddy bears are silly.

2. Why couldn't the child in the poem fall asleep?

    A. The child was cold.

    B. The child was worried that the parents were angry.

    C. The child was hungry.

    D. The child thought that the teddy bear was afraid.

3. What did the child do when there was a storm?

    A. got the teddy bear   B. went into Mom and Dad's room

    C. cried   D. hid under the covers

4. **Kid** and **hid** are words that rhyme in the poem. Which two words in the pairs below do not rhyme?

    A. **fun** and **run**   B. **bike** and **ride**

    C. **bear** and **tear**   D. **hide** and **side**

5. **Asleep** and **peep** are words in the poem that make the long **e** sound. Which word below does not have the long **e** sound?

    A. read   B. see

    C. agree   D. bed

© Carson-Dellosa

Write the missing letters ou or ow for each word.

1.

cl_____ _____d

2.

m_____ _____th

3.

_____ _____l

4.

cl_____ _____n

5.

p_____ _____nd

6.

pl_____ _____

Follow the directions to solve each problem.

7. Start with 700. Write the number that is 100 less. _____

8. Start with 600. Write the number that is 300 less. _____

9. Start with 200. Write the number that is 200 less. _____

10. Start with 800. Write the number that is 500 less. _____

11. Start with 900. Write the number that is 400 less. _____

12. Start with 500. Write the number that is 100 less. _____

© Carson-Dellosa

Complete.

1.

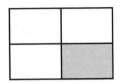

There are ___4___ equal parts.

___1___ of the parts is shaded.

___1/4___ of the whole is shaded.

2.

There are _____ equal parts.

_____ of the parts is shaded.

___—___ of the whole is shaded.

Write the fraction that is shaded in words.

3.

___One-half___ is shaded.

4.

_____ is shaded.

Say each word aloud. Write the syllables in the boxes.

5. handwriting

6. enormous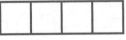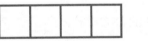

7. subtraction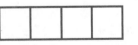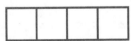

8. principal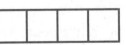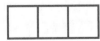

© Carson-Dellosa

Read each sentence. If the underlined word is spelled correctly, circle yes. If the underlined word is not spelled correctly, circle no.

1. Uma has a very <u>smoll</u> kitten.   yes   no

2. The United States flag is red, white, and <u>blue</u>.   yes   no

3. Those girls were in my <u>class</u>.   yes   no

4. Gina is a very <u>helpfull</u> friend.   yes   no

5. I made this by <u>myslef</u>.   yes   no

6. This glue is sticky <u>stuf</u>.   yes   no

7. Can you <u>moov</u> your arm?   yes   no

Write the expanded form for each number.

EXAMPLE:

643 = __6__ hundreds + __4__ tens + __3__ ones = **600** + **40** + **3**

8. 237 = ____ hundreds + ____ tens + ____ ones = ____ + ____ + ____

9. 422 = ____ hundreds + ____ tens + ____ ones = ____ + ____ + ____

10. 781 = ____ hundreds + ____ tens + ____ one = ____ + ____ + ____

11. 965 = ____ hundreds + ____ tens + ____ ones = ____ + ____ + ____

FITNESS FLASH: Stretch in child's pose. Kneel on a soft surface and sit back on your feet. Slowly bend forward at the waist and rest your forehead on the floor.

© Carson-Dellosa

Complete.

1.

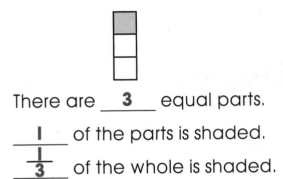

There are ___3___ equal parts.

___1___ of the parts is shaded.

$\dfrac{1}{3}$ of the whole is shaded.

2.

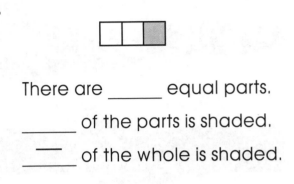

There are _____ equal parts.

_____ of the parts is shaded.

___—___ of the whole is shaded.

Write the fraction that is shaded in words.

3.

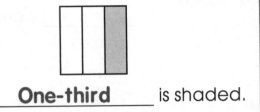

__One-third__ is shaded.

4.

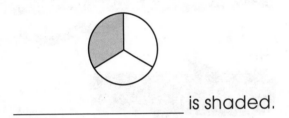

_____ is shaded.

Pronouns take the place of nouns. A reflexive pronoun is a special type of pronoun that ends in –self or –selves. Circle the reflexive pronoun in each sentence.

5.   We put on a play all by ourselves!

6.   The boys were proud of themselves for passing the test.

7.   You know yourself better than anyone else does.

8.   Rafael tried to teach himself to play guitar.

9.   I told myself not to be scared as I entered the dark room.

© Carson-Dellosa

Use a ruler to measure each branch to the nearest centimeter.

1.

= _____ centimeters

2.

= _____ centimeters

3.

= _____ centimeters

4.

= _____ centimeters

Write > (greater than) or < (less than) to compare each pair of numbers.

5. 103 ◯ 303

6. 458 ◯ 460

7. 110 ◯ 100

8. 190 ◯ 910

9. 290 ◯ 300

10. 985 ◯ 850

11. 140 ◯ 410

12. 214 ◯ 216

13. 648 ◯ 804

14. 360 ◯ 480

15. 592 ◯ 324

16. 745 ◯ 475

© Carson-Dellosa

Solve each problem.

> **EXAMPLE:**
> Case left for ball practice at 3:00.   Think: 3:00 + 0:20 = 3:20
> His walk took 20 minutes.
> What time did Case get to practice?

1. Ellen ate breakfast at 7:00. She ate a snack 2 hours later. What time did she eat her snack?

   _____

2. This morning, Hau read for 15 minutes. He started at 9:00. What time did he finish reading?

   _____

3. The movie lasted an hour and 30 minutes. It started at 6:00. What time did it end?

   _____

4. Ellis left school at 3:30. He rode the bus for 30 minutes. What time did he get off of the bus?

   _____

Circle each pronoun in the sentences below. Include reflexive pronouns.

5. Nate reminded himself to call Sabrina on Monday.

6. He needed to tell her about a club meeting.

7. It started at 4:00.

8. "We can walk there ourselves," he thought.

© Carson-Dellosa

Circle the word that is spelled correctly in each row.

1. do'nt   don'nt   don't
2. esy   easy   eazy
3. lauf   laugh   laff
4. boys   bois   boies
5. briht   bright   brigte
6. wonce   onse   once
7. carry   carey   carre
8. hurt   hirt   hert
9. star   stor   starr
10. peeple   people   peple

Continue each pattern by drawing 3 more pictures.

11.

| 1 | 2 | 3 | 4 |

2   4   6   8

12.

CHARACTER CHECK: Plan a schedule for the day. Write each hour down the left side of a sheet of paper. Then, write next to each hour what you plan to do at that time.

© Carson-Dellosa

Use the hundreds, tens, and ones blocks to help you solve each problem.

1. 243
    + 126

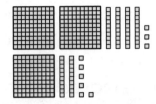

2. 542
    + 437

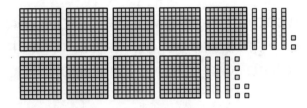

3. 595
    − 222

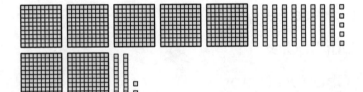

Write about a time when you felt proud. What made you feel that way?

_____

_____

_____

_____

_____

_____

© Carson-Dellosa

Read the passage. Then, answer the questions.

Chemicals

Chemicals are everywhere. They make up our air, our houses, our food, and even our bodies. Chemicals help make everything different. They make apples sweet and lemons sour. They make leaves green in spring and red, orange, and yellow in fall.

When chemicals mix to form something new, it is called a *reaction*. As a banana ripens, it changes from green to yellow. This is from chemicals changing. When you mix chocolate with milk, you are watching chemicals change in a tasty way!

1. A good title for this passage would be:

    A. Chemicals in Our Bodies

    B. Why Bananas Change Color

    C. Chemicals Around Us

2. What is the main idea of first paragraph?

    A. Apples are sweet.

    B. Chemicals are everywhere.

    C. Leaves are green.

3. What is the main idea of second paragraph?

    A. Chemicals can cause changes.

    B. Bananas turn from green to yellow.

    C. Chocolate milk is tasty.

 REMINDER: Did you write down activities you want to do before summer is over? Have you made any of those things happen?

© Carson-Dellosa

Moss Garden

Create a beautiful miniature garden out of living moss!

Start by going on a moss hunt with an adult. Look for moss in shady, moist places. It could be growing on rocks, trees, walls, lawns, or even porch steps. Carefully dig up small pieces of moss. Then, follow these directions to transplant your moss into your indoor garden.

Materials:
- A shallow (about 2 inches deep) planting tray without drainage holes
- Gravel or crushed stone
- Potting soil
- Spray bottle of water
- Moss
- Stones, leaves, twigs, or other decorative objects from nature

Procedure:
1. Cover the bottom of the planting tray with a layer of gravel. This will allow water to drain away from the moss and soil.
2. Add about $\frac{1}{2}$ inch of potting soil on top of the gravel. Spray the soil with water so that it is moist, but not wet.
3. Arrange the moss on top of the potting soil. Play with the position of each piece until you are happy with how it looks.
4. Use the stones, leaves, twigs, etc. to decorate your garden.

Spray your moss with water once a day. Twice a week, you should water it like any other plant—just be sure not to add too much water. Your moss should keep growing in your garden as long as it's getting what it needs.

NOTE:
Some types of moss grow in sunny places, too, but to make sure you can make your moss feel at home inside, it's better to find the kinds that like shade.

© Carson-Dellosa

Acting Games

This is for You

Play with one or more friends. Find an empty box that can be opened and closed easily. Feel free to wrap it like a present. If you don't have a box, you can just pretend. In this game, a gift giver and a gift receiver will have a conversation about what is in the box.

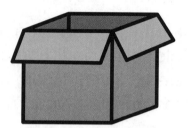

Two people take the stage. One person (the giver) gives the box to the other, and says, "This is for you" without saying what is in the box. It is the receiver's job to decide what the gift is and respond to it. The receiver has to give enough information about the gift to keep the conversation going. Here's an example of how a conversation might go:

GIVER: This is for you! I thought of you when I saw it and just had to get it.

RECEIVER: Wow! Thank you! I've always wanted a baby hippopotamus!

GIVER: I'm so glad! I mean, I knew you loved hippos, but I wasn't sure you would have room in your house for one.

RECEIVER: It'll be fine. How much space could this little guy need?

Varying Voices

Play with one or more friends. Choose some favorite stuffed animals, and place them in a group. Then, cut strips of paper and write a person or place on each one. Include people like **bus driver**, **baby**, and **president** and places like **library**, **amusement park**, and **restaurant**. Fold up the slips, and put the people in one container and the places in another.

When it is your turn, take a slip from each container. Then, choose a stuffed animal from the group to represent the person on the slip. Speak to the stuffed animal in the tone of voice and volume appropriate for both the person and the place. The other player(s) should try to guess where you are and whom you are speaking to.

© Carson-Dellosa

Write an addition equation to find the total number of items in each picture.

EXAMPLE:

$$3 + 3 + 3 + 3 = 12$$

1.

2.

_____

3.

4.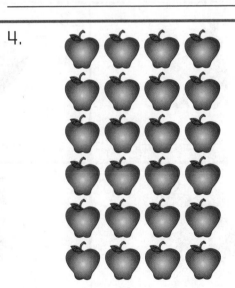

_____

© Carson-Dellosa

Write the word from the box that names each picture.

auto	yawn	stew	hood	faucet	fawn
laundry	screw	tooth	claw	book	moose

1.
_____

2.
_____

3.
_____

4.
_____

5.
_____

6.
_____

7.
_____

8.
_____

9.
_____

10.
_____

11.
_____

12.
_____

© Carson-Dellosa

Write the best adjective from the box to complete each sentence. An adjective is a word that describes a person, place, or thing.

| happy | fluffy | hard | pine | blue | nine |

1. His kite got caught in that _____ tree.

2. I cannot believe you ate _____ slices of watermelon.

3. Mom was so _____ to see us.

4. My tongue turned _____ from the cotton candy.

5. My pillow is very _____ and lumpy.

6. The rabbits all have soft and _____ fur.

Repeated addition problems help you get ready for multiplication. Add to find each sum.

7.   2
     2
  + 2

8.   3
     3
  + 3

9.   4
     4
  + 4

10.   5
      5
   + 5

11.   2
      2
      2
   + 2

12.   3
      3
      3
   + 3

13.   4
      4
      4
   + 4

14.   5
      5
      5
   + 5

© Carson-Dellosa

Read the passage.

Twins

Greg and Tim are twins. They are brothers who were born on the same day. Twins that look almost exactly alike are called identical twins. Greg and Tim do look somewhat alike, but they are not identical twins. Greg and Tim are fraternal twins. That means they were born on the same day but do not look exactly alike.

Tim has curly red hair. Greg's hair is brown and straight. Greg has green eyes. Tim's eyes are blue. Another difference between them right now is their teeth. Greg is missing his two front teeth. Tim has all of his teeth, and he has braces!

Both boys like to play baseball. Sometimes, they play third base. Sometimes, they play catcher. Both of them can throw the ball well. It can be fun to have a twin.

© Carson-Dellosa

Answer the questions about the passage on page 174. Read each phrase. If it describes Greg, write a G on the line. If it describes Tim, write a T on the line. If the phrase describes both boys, write a B on the line.

1. _____ is a twin

2. _____ has red hair

3. _____ plays catcher

4. _____ missing two front teeth

5. _____ has green eyes

6. Draw a picture of each boy.

7. What do you call twins that do not look exactly alike?

_____

8. Circle the words below that have a long vowel sound.

twin	red	base
teeth	play	fun
braces	Tim	both

© Carson-Dellosa

Summertime Song, Step 2

Every song needs a beat! Build this drum to play as you write and perform your summer song.

Materials:

- Coffee can with a plastic lid
- Construction paper
- Crayons, markers, or paint
- Tape
- Scissors

© Carson-Dellosa

Directions:

1. Cut the construction paper to fit around the coffee can.

2. Decorate your paper.

3. Cover the can with the paper, and tape it on.

4. Beat rhythms on the lid with your hands.

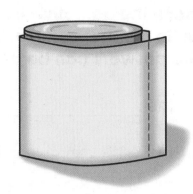

Suggestion:
Fill a one-pound coffee can with water. Stretch an inner tube over the top tied on tightly with heavy rubber bands. This drum makes a wonderful sound.

© Carson-Dellosa

Choose the adjective from the second column that best describes each noun in the first column. Write the letter of the adjective on the line. Some answers can be used twice.

1. the _____ sunshine   a. green

2. the _____ bird   b. rough

3. the _____ grass   c. chirping

4. the _____ squirrel   d. warm

5. the _____ bark of the tree   e. noisy

6. the _____ lawnmower   f. furry

Pack Your Own Lunch!

Impress your family by making your own lunch! Try this recipe at home for a healthy yet delicious school lunch.

Mini Pizza Pitas
4 mini whole-wheat pitas (or one large pita, cut into triangles)
3 TBS pizza sauce
$\frac{1}{4}$ cup shredded mozzarella cheese
Side of fruit

Carefully spoon pizza sauce into a small airtight container. Then, using a multi-sectioned plastic container, place the pitas in one section, cheese in another, and the side of fruit in the last. At lunchtime, assemble your mini pizzas, and enjoy!

© Carson-Dellosa

Draw same-size squares 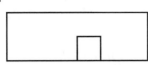 **to fill each rectangle. Then, count the number of squares.**

1.
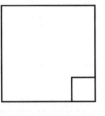

_____ square units

2.

_____ square units

3.
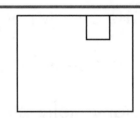

_____ square units

4.

_____ square units

5.

_____ square units

6.

_____ square units

Write the new word.

7. slide + ing = _____

8. stretch + ing = _____

9. move + ing = _____

10. snow + ing = _____

11. make + ing = _____

12. dry + ing = _____

 REMINDER: Have you been doing any of your favorite summer activities? Make sure to keep track on page 151, and try to get pictures of the beginning, middle, and end of each event.

© Carson-Dellosa

Circle the adverb in each sentence. Then, decide if the adverb tells when, where, or how. Write when, where, or how on the line beside the sentence.

1. Yesterday, it snowed. _____

2. Big flakes fell gently to the ground. _____

3. Ian looked everywhere for his mittens. _____

4. He quickly put on his boots and hat. _____

5. He opened the door and walked outside. _____

6. Ian quietly listened to the snow falling. _____

Complete each number pattern. Write the rule.

7. 6, 8, 10, 12, _____, _____, _____, _____, _____, _____

    Rule: _____

8. 20, 30, 40, _____, _____, _____, _____, _____, _____

    Rule: _____

9. 5, 10, 15, _____, _____, _____, _____, _____, _____

    Rule: _____

10. 6, 9, 12, 15, _____, _____, _____, _____, _____, _____

    Rule: _____

© Carson-Dellosa

Use a ruler to measure the logs to the nearest inch. Then, show the measurements on the line plot. For each log, draw an X above the number that shows its measurement.

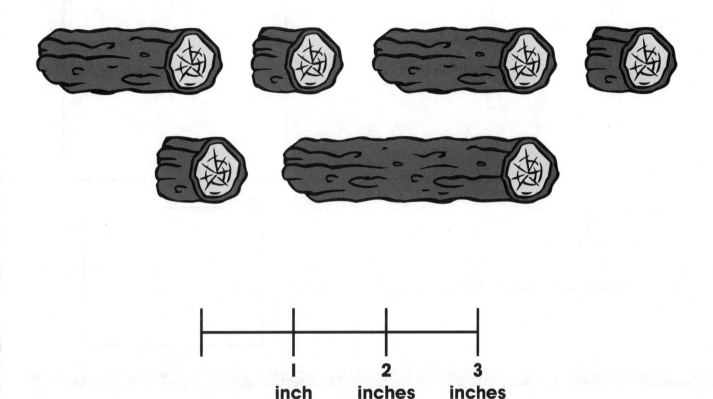

```
        |-------|-------|-------|
        I       I       2       3
      inch   inches  inches
```

Read each pair of sentences. Find a word in the first sentence that makes sense in the second sentence. Write the word on the line.

1. Jabar planted carrots in his garden.

   His sister loved to eat _____.

2. It was a relief to finish the test.

   It was a _____ to get a good grade.

© Carson-Dellosa

Draw lines to divide each rectangle into rows and columns. Then, count how many squares there are. Write your answer on the line.

1. 4 rows
   5 columns

   How many squares? _____

2. 3 rows
   4 columns

   How many squares? _____

Use the unfinished sentence below to start a story. Use your imagination and be as descriptive as possible.

The door creaked slowly open, and I could see . . .

_____

_____

_____

_____

_____

© Carson-Dellosa

Write Your Own Ending

Read the story, and then decide how you want it to end.

Larry the Lion had been king of the grasslands for a very long time. But, the animals felt that they needed a new king. King Larry had become lazy, mean, and selfish. When King Larry learned of how the animals felt, he set them free and laughed to himself, "They will beg to have me back!" The animals did not beg to have Larry back, and so he moved away.

One lonely day, Larry found a mouse that was balancing on a branch over the river. He helped the mouse to the shore. Later, Larry found a baby zebra who was lost. Larry was kind and helped the little zebra find his home.

Directions:

Now, write your own ending to the story on a separate sheet of paper. What do you think happens next? Is the ending happy or sad? Then, draw a picture to go with your ending. Make it match the most important moment at the end of the story. Finally, give the story a title that fits.

© Carson-Dellosa

Make a Box Guitar!

You can make a guitar with things you have around the house. You'll be strumming tunes in no time!

Materials:

- A shoebox (no lid needed)
- Rubber bands of varying widths
- Tempera paint
- Paintbrushes with stiff bristles
- Paper towel roll
- Glue

© Carson-Dellosa

Directions:

1. Paint the paper towel roll and entire shoebox, a few sides at a time, with a dark brown color. Let it dry.

2. Paint over the dark brown with lighter brown paint. This makes it look like wood. Let it dry.

3. Glue the paper towel roll to a short end of the shoebox.

4. Stretch rubber bands around the open shoebox. Space them out evenly, from the widest to the narrowest band.

5. Experiment by plucking the strings one at a time as well as by strumming the strings all at once.

Find a friend and play this game.

The Great Race

What You Will Need:
- Coin
- Space Markers

Object of the Game:
To be the first to cross the finish line

How to Play:
The youngest player goes first.

Flip a coin. Move one space for heads. Move two spaces for tails. Follow the directions on each space.

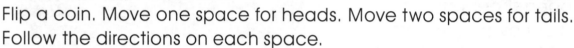

Start	Slow start. Go back 1 space.	Great start! Go ahead 2 spaces.			Tripped on shoelace. Go back 1 space.	
			Running strong. Take another turn.			
	Record time. Go ahead 3 spaces.		Record time. Go ahead 3 spaces.			
				Getting tired. Go back 3 spaces.		
	Missed a hurdle. Go back 2 spaces.					**Finish**

© Carson-Dellosa

Answer the questions about the activity on page 186.

1. What is the main idea?

    A. how to play a game

    B. how to run in a race

    C. how to be in first place

2. Who goes first?

    A. the owner of the game

    B. the biggest person

    C. the youngest person

3. What is the object of the game?

    A. to not trip when running a race

    B. to be the first to cross the finish line

    C. to get the best start

4. What is the consequence of each action?

    A. tripped on shoelace

    _____

    B. getting tired

    _____

    C. missed a hurdle

    _____

Read this game box. Answer the questions below.

A Rainbow Bridge Game

Hop to It!

The game that keeps you on your toes

For 3 or more players
For ages 5 to adult

5. What is the game's name?

    _____

6. How old do you need to be to

    play the game? _____

7. Can two people play the

    game? _____

Write the base word for the following words:

8. tripped _____

9. running _____

10. getting _____

11. tired _____

12. crossed _____

© Carson-Dellosa

Use the number line to help you solve each problem. Mark the number line to show your work.

1. 40 + 35 = _____

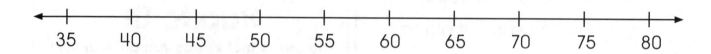

```
35    40    45    50    55    60    65    70    75    80
```

2. 80 – 50 = _____

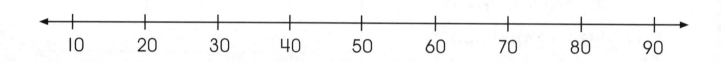

```
10    20    30    40    50    60    70    80    90
```

Use the words in the balloons one time each to complete the sentences.

smile

clown

balloons

laugh

3. My uncle's job is to be a circus _____.

4. He paints a big, red _____ on his face.

5. He makes animals by blowing up and tying _____.

6. He goes to parties and makes children _____.

FACTOID: One inch of rain can make about 10 inches of snow!

© Carson-Dellosa

Choose the correct adverb from the words in parentheses ( ). Write it in the blank.

1. Ian _____ ran to his friend Ming's house. (quickly, quick)

2. He knocked _____ at the back door. (loud, loudly)

3. _____ , Ming was ready to play in the snow. (Soon, Sooner)

4. Ming's brother, Jin, came home _____ . (early, earliest)

5. He _____ joined Ming and Ian in the yard. (happy, happily)

6. _____ , they built a snowman. (Then, Last)

Use the mileage maps to answer the questions.

7. How many miles is it from Fairmont to Topsfield? _____

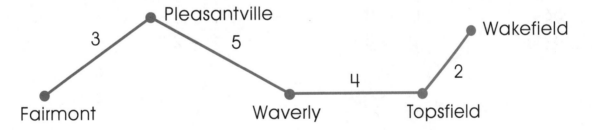

8. How many miles is it from Jackson to Lodi? _____

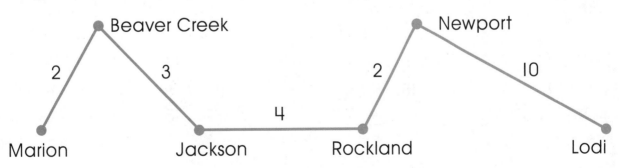

© Carson-Dellosa

Cross out the word that does not belong in each group.

1. apple banana potato watermelon	2. whale bobcat squirrel raccoon	3. boat car airplane road	4. boots hat mittens snowman
5. towel soap shampoo shoes	6. cotton rock pillow feather	7. candle flashlight mirror lantern	8. bitter sour lemon sweet

Add or subtract to solve each problem.

9. 56
   + 37

10. 48
   + 35

11. 63
   + 28

12. 88
   + 12

13. 27
   + 57

14. 59
   + 28

15. 70
   − 18

16. 81
   − 22

17. 67
   − 33

18. 54
   − 17

19. 82
   − 56

20. 71
   − 38

© Carson-Dellosa

Count the money for each problem. Write how much money is shown.

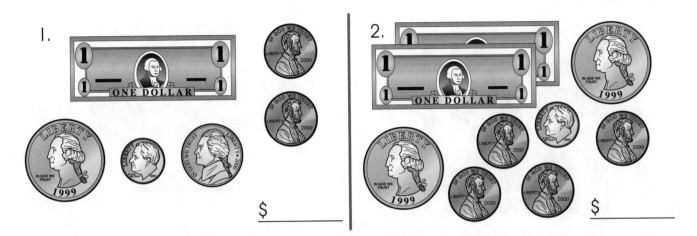

I.

$ _____

2.

$ _____

Use the words from the box to complete each analogy. An analogy is a way to show how things are alike. To complete an analogy, look at the first set of words. Decide how they are related. Apply that relationship to the second set of words.

EXAMPLE: *Finger : hand :: toe : _____*. (A *finger* is part of a *hand*. What is a *toe* a part of? The answer is *foot*.)

large	sky	square	ball

3.   jump : rope :: toss : _____

4.   three : triangle :: four : _____

5.   green : grass :: blue : _____

6.   open : close :: small : _____

FACTOID: If you jumped rope for an hour straight, your body would burn about half the calories you need for the day!

© Carson-Dellosa

Use a ruler to measure the sides of each shape to the nearest inch. Then, add.

1.

2.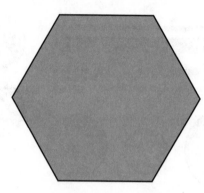

____ + ____ + ____ + ____ = ____   ___ + ___ + ___ + ___ + ___ + ___ = ___

Read the table of contents. Write the chapter and page number of where you should begin looking for the answer to each question.

The Cool-Kids' Cookbook
Table of Contents

3. How do you make scrambled eggs?   Chapter ____ Page ____

4. What should I serve at my party?   Chapter ____ Page ____

5. How long does a layer cake need to bake? Chapter ____ Page ____

6. What are some good picnic foods?   Chapter ____ Page ____

© Carson-Dellosa

Write a or an in front of each noun.

1. _____ career

2. _____ operation

3. _____ doctor

4. _____ scientist

5. _____ actor

6. _____ effort

7. _____ artist

8. _____ railroad

Use the prices for the snacks below to write each subtraction problem. Find the answer.

$2.38 $1.29 $1.38 $1.34

9. Mr. Smith bought a hot dog during the play. He paid with $3.00. How much change will he get?

10. How much more does popcorn cost than soda?

11. What is the difference in price between a hot dog and a soda?

12. Erin bought a soda. She paid with $1.50. How much change will she get?

© Carson-Dellosa

Add or subtract to solve each problem.

1. 66
   + 24

2. 28
   + 37

3. 73
   + 18

4. 42
   + 33

5. 19
   + 54

6. 39
   + 26

7. 42
   − 28

8. 90
   − 27

9. 44
   − 22

10. 58
   − 34

11. 74
   − 36

12. 83
   − 18

Write about something you did with your friends recently. Use at least two of these adverbs in your description: slowly, quickly, loudly, quietly, suddenly, before, later, after, sometimes.

_____

_____

_____

_____

FITNESS FLASH: See how fast you can move on all fours! Time yourself as you "run" from your bedroom to the front door.

© Carson-Dellosa

Keegan wanted to know how many ants would come to a pile of sugar in five minutes. Each minute, he counted the number of ants at the sugar pile. Look at the graph to see Keegan's findings. Then, answer the questions.

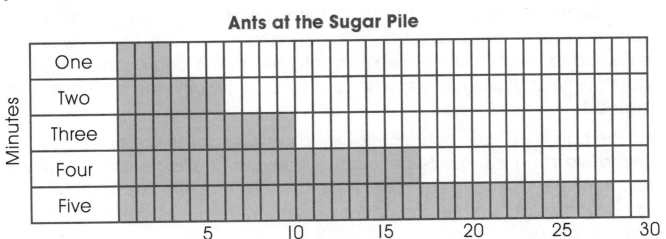

Ants at the Sugar Pile

1. How many ants came to the sugar pile in the first minute? _____

2. How many ants arrived between the second and third minutes? _____

3. How many ants arrived between the fourth and fifth minutes? _____

4. How many ants had arrived by the fifth minute? _____

5. Between which two minutes did the most ants arrive? _____

6. If Keegan had graphed the sixth minute, do you think the number of

   ants would have gone up or down? Explain. _____

   _____

   _____

© Carson-Dellosa

Read the story. Then, follow the directions.

City Mouse, Country Mouse

Once upon a time, a city mouse went to visit her friend in the country. The country mouse spent the day gathering grain and dried pieces of corn in order to greet her friend with a nice meal. The city mouse was surprised to find her friend living in a cold tree stump and eating scraps. So, she invited the country mouse to visit her in the city. The country mouse agreed.

The country mouse could not believe her eyes when she arrived! Her friend lived in a warm hole behind the fireplace of a large home. She was even more surprised to find all of the fine foods that were left behind after a party the night before. The country mouse wished that she could live in the city as well.

Suddenly, the family's cat ran in and chased the two mice. He nearly caught the country mouse with his sharp claws. As the friends raced back to the mouse hole, the country mouse said, "I'm sorry, friend, but I would rather live a simple life eating corn and grain than live a fancy life in fear!" The country mouse went back home.

The two characters in this story are different from each other. Mark an X in each box to describe the correct mouse.

	City Mouse	Country Mouse
I. She feasted on fine foods.		
2. She would rather have a simple, safe life.		
3. She gathered grain and corn.		
4. She lived in a large house.		
5. She was surprised by all of the fine foods.		
6. She lived in a warm place.		

FACTOID: A baby mouse is called a pinky.

© Carson-Dellosa

Mud Painting

Materials:

Small pile of dirt (Shake free any rocks, grass, or other objects.)

Water

Bucket

Paintbrush—about 1 inch wide

Light-colored outdoor surface—such as a sidewalk or porch steps

Directions:

Step One: In the bucket, mix the dirt with water, adding just a little bit at a time until your mud is thin like tempera paint. It should feel smooth when you stir it, as if it would be easy to paint with.

Step Two: Once your mud is ready, try painting some words you know or solving some math problems. You might even try telling a story with words or pictures.

Have fun, and don't be afraid to experiment! Here are some other things you might like to mud paint:

- Names of friends and family
- Clues for a treasure hunt
- Today's weather report
- Directions to the park
- Road signs you know
- Map of your state
- 3D shapes
- Tic Tac Toe
- Hopscotch
- Hangman

© Carson-Dellosa

Take It Outside!

Go outside and lie down on your side in the grass. Imagine what your life would be like if you were shorter than a blade of grass. What would bugs and animals look like to you? What about humans? What would you eat? How would you get around? Write a journal entry that shows what it's like to be you for a day. Draw a picture to go with it.

Ask an adult family member for a sock that is no longer needed. Put the sock over your shoe. Go outside and walk through tall grass or bushes. Take the sock off and shake it over a piece of paper to see if you collected any seeds. How many different kinds of seeds did you get?

Gather ten different sticks outside. First, put them in order starting with the shortest stick and ending with the longest. Then, put them in order starting with the thinnest stick and ending with the thickest stick. Finally, line them all up end to end and see how long they stretch. Measure with a measuring tape.

© Carson-Dellosa

Summertime Song, Step 3

You've had your adventures. You've made your drum. Now, it's time to choose the adventures you want to put to music!

First, go back to your list of summer adventures on page 143. Cross off anything that didn't happen yet this summer. Then, choose at least two events to use in your song. You might pick the events that were the most exciting or the most important to you. Or, you might choose things that scared you, made you laugh, or made you proud. Whatever you choose, make sure you have plenty to say about it.

Use the space below to write down all the important details you can remember about the adventures you want to sing about. Continue on a separate sheet of paper, if needed.

_____

_____

_____

_____

_____

_____

_____

_____

© Carson-Dellosa

Summer Adventures Picture Book, Step 3

Return to this month's summer adventures on page 151, and review your list of favorite activities on page 144. Cross anything off the list that did not happen this summer. Then, choose three adventures to turn into a picture book. Which events give you the most to talk about? Which ones feel the most like a story? Choose those, and then answer the questions below. Continue on a separate sheet of paper, if needed.

Adventure 1: _____

What happened in the beginning? _____

What happened in the middle? _____

What happened in the end? _____

Adventure 2: _____

What happened in the beginning? _____

What happened in the middle? _____

What happened in the end? _____

Adventure 3: _____

What happened in the beginning? _____

What happened in the middle? _____

What happened in the end? _____

© Carson-Dellosa

Add to find each sum.

1. 200
   + 162

2. 882
   + 100

3. 500
   + 391

4. 782
   + 200

5. 400
   + 321

6. 862
   + 100

7. 500
   + 130

8. 720
   + 200

9. 400
   + 111

10. 823
    + 100

11. 461
    + 400

12. 762
    + 200

13. 500
    + 250

14. 382
    + 300

15. 600
    + 305

Take Charge of Your Learning!

Think about one subject or skill you would like to improve in this year.
Name three people who can help you do that.

Subject or Skill: _____

Who Can Help:

1. _____

2. _____

3. _____

© Carson-Dellosa

Read the sentences. If the underlined word is an adjective, write adj. on the line. If it is an adverb, write adv. on the line.

1. _____ <u>Yesterday</u>, Carlos and Grandpa walked to the pool.

2. _____ The day was <u>hot</u>.

3. _____ The <u>blue</u> water was cool to touch.

4. _____ Carlos and Grandpa <u>quickly</u> jumped in the pool.

5. _____ Carlos loved swimming in the <u>cool</u> water.

6. _____ Grandpa <u>easily</u> swam a few laps.

Read each question. Circle the correct answer. Then, draw the shape in the box.

7. I have three sides and three angles. What am I?

   A. a quadrilateral

   B. a triangle

   C. a hexagon

8. I am a quadrilateral with four equal sides. My opposite sides and opposite angles are equal. What am I?

   A. a rhombus

   B. a triangle

   C. a pentagon

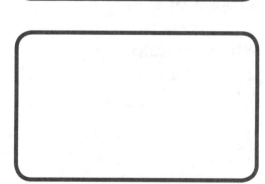

© Carson-Dellosa

Subtract to find each difference.

YOU MADE IT!

849 − 300	643 − 200

542 − 300

947 − 600

747 − 300

859 − 300

738 − 500

698 − 400

695 − 200

547 − 300

989 − 600

496 − 100

START

CHARACTER CHECK: Write three ways your first day of school will be a success.

© Carson-Dellosa

Use this map and map key with page 205.

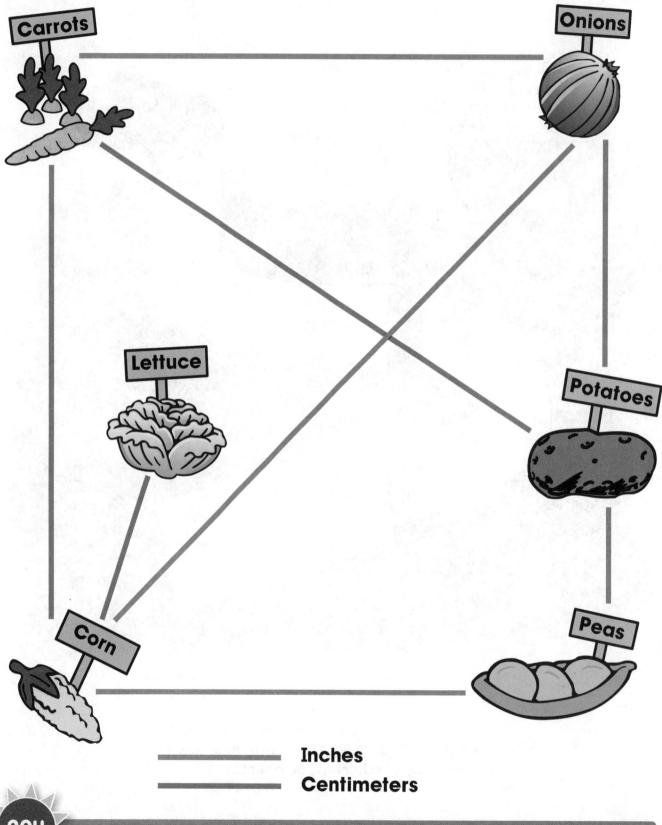

Carrots

Onions

Lettuce

Potatoes

Corn

Peas

_____ Inches

_____ Centimeters

© Carson-Dellosa

Iggy the Lizard and Slinky the Salamander are feasting in the garden. Measure their paths on page 204. Measure Iggy's path with inches. Iggy's path is the blue line. Measure Slinky's path with centimeters. Slinky's path is the red line. Then, write each length to the nearest inch or centimeter.

Iggy's Inches		Slinky's Centimeters	
Start at		Start at	
Go to	in.	Go to	cm
Go to	in.	Go to	cm
Go to	in.	Go to	cm
Last to	in.	Last to	cm
Total	in.	Total	cm

© Carson-Dellosa

Read the passage.

Changing with the Seasons

Humans are not the only ones to change our clothes with the seasons. We change the way we dress with the seasons to protect us from the weather. Animals do the same thing to protect themselves from the weather. They know when the weather will change.

For example, the arctic fox has a thick, white fur coat in the winter. It is not easy to see in the snow. This helps the fox to hide from enemies. When spring comes, the fox's fur changes to brown. It is then the color of the ground.

The Ptarmigan bird, or White Chicken, has white feathers in the winter. It, too, is hard to see in the snow. In the spring, the bird molts. This means that it sheds all of its feathers. The bird grows new feathers that are speckled. When the bird is very still, it looks like a rock.

© Carson-Dellosa

Answer the questions about the passage on page 206.

1. What is "Changing with the Seasons" mostly about?

   A. how people change

   B. how seasons change

   C. how animals change with the seasons

2. What color is the arctic fox's fur in the winter?

   A. brown

   B. white

   C. black

3. What happens to the Ptarmigan bird in the spring?

   A. It molts.

   B. It flies south.

   C. Its feathers turn red.

4. The word **molts** means:

   A. to change colors.

   B. to shed feathers.

   C. to hide from an enemy.

5. Draw a line to divide the two words that make up each compound word.

   A. springtime

   B. wintertime

   C. bluebird

6. What words could you type into a search engine or look up in a book to read more about how animals change each season?

   _____

   _____

   _____

FITNESS FLASH: Try plank pose. Start on your hands and knees, and then straighten your legs and make your whole body straight like a plank of wood. Keep your shoulders directly above your wrists, and tighten your stomach muscles.

© Carson-Dellosa

Use the chart to answer each question.

Allowance for Each Chore Completed

Pull weeds	$3.00
Take out trash	$1.25
Put away groceries	$0.75
Wash the car	$5.00
Hang up laundry	$1.00

1. Which chore pays the least money? _____

2. If Sarah hangs up laundry every day this week, how much will she earn? _____

3. Brack washed the car three times this month. How much money did he earn? _____

Read the paragraphs. Circle each adjective you find. Underline each adverb. There are six adjectives and five adverbs.

Carlos was taking a nap on the long, plastic chair. Suddenly, he heard a loud noise. He felt a drop of cold water on his face. Carlos thought his friend was playfully splashing him. Grandpa stood beside Carlos.

"We should quickly find shelter," said Grandpa. Very big raindrops started to fall from the stormy sky. Carlos and Grandpa ran inside.

© Carson-Dellosa

A glossary is found at the back of a book. It tells what certain words in the book mean. Use this glossary from a book about deserts to answer the questions.

captivity the keeping of animals someplace other than the wild
carnivore an animal that eats other animals
ecosystem all the living things in a certain place that depend on each other to survive
instincts ways of thinking or acting that an animal does not have to learn
stalk to creep up on an animal without being seen or heard

1. What does **carnivore** mean? _____

2. A bird uses its _____ to build a nest.

3. Tigers and other cats _____ other animals.

4. What is an example of a place that keeps animals in captivity?

   _____

Add or subtract to solve each problem.

5.	71 + 29	6.	76 + 12	7.	38 − 32	8.	92 − 75	9.	89 + 10

10.	583 − 400	11.	710 − 200	12.	582 + 400	13.	711 − 500	14.	712 − 100

© Carson-Dellosa

Use what you know about money to solve each problem.

 Zach has 3 quarters. Does he have enough to buy a book for 80¢?

He has ___75¢___.   Yes   (No)

1. Tom has 2 quarters and 1 dime. Does he have enough money to buy a toy truck that costs 75¢?

    He has _____¢

    Yes   No

2. Jane has 3 dimes and 4 nickels. Does she have enough to buy a toy that costs 25¢?

    She has _____¢

    Yes   No

Write a paragraph about your favorite book or movie. Include details about why it is your favorite. Your first sentence should include the title. Your last sentence should sum up your opinion.

_____

_____

_____

_____

_____

© Carson-Dellosa

Summertime Song, Final Step

It's time to write your Summertime Song!

Using the drum you made on page 176, write lyrics and music for a song about something you experienced this summer. Try to write at least two verses and a chorus. Then, practice your song and perform it for your friends and family.

Materials:

- drum
- chosen adventures from page 199
- paper and pencil

Directions:

1. Take the details you wrote about your chosen adventures, and brainstorm ideas for lyrics. You might want to begin with a drum beat and see what words come to you. Or, begin by writing lyrics and then add the beat to fit the words. It might help ideas to flow if you walk or dance around as you try out the lines for your song. And, remember, you don't have to sing; you can just chant!

2. Decide how your song will start. Will it begin with the chorus or the first verse? How many times will you repeat the chorus and at what points?

3. Once you've got the lyrics, practice singing or chanting the words as you drum.

4. When you're ready, invite friends and family to your performance. You might even ask others to grab instruments and join your band. Someone could play the box guitar you made on page 184!

5. If possible, record the performance and send a link to out-of-town friends and family.

© Carson-Dellosa

Summertime Song
Finished Product Example

Here's an example of some summertime song lyrics. But, it's just an example—your song might look very different. You decide how long each line should be, how many lines per verse, and how many verses total. And, of course, don't forget to add the beat!

CHORUS
Running, swimming, playing ball
Hide 'N' Seek and free-for-alls
Hotdogs, ice cream, cherry pie
Watermelon, bright blue skies
All this was fun, but here's the truth
The best was my blue bathing suit

VERSE 1
I wore my blue suit to the pool
Took swimming lessons, feeling cool
In just one day I passed the test
Swam up and back without a rest!
Then, I climbed that diving board
Took the plunge, and the whole crowd roared!

VERSE 2
I wore my blue suit to the beach
Swam out to where I couldn't reach
Jumped on the float with the waterslide
My dad and I, we took a ride
Flew down the slide and made a splash
"I'll race you back!" I said, then dashed!

© Carson-Dellosa

Summer Adventures Picture Book, Final Step

You're ready to write your picture book! Follow the directions below.

Materials:
- your three favorite adventures from page 200
- the pictures of your three favorite adventures
- plain white sheets of paper (You will use both sides of each sheet)
- markers, colored pencils, or crayons
- pencil or pen
- glue or tape
- stapler

Directions:
1. Review the beginning, middle, and end of each adventure from page 200. What details could you add to make each part fun to read about? You might describe the setting, an important person, or specific actions in more detail. Consider using dialogue (what people say) to show what was happening at a particular moment.

2. Look at your pictures for each of your chosen events. Decide which words of your story go with which pictures. Then, if you need more pictures to make your story come to life, draw them.

3. Give each of your adventures a title. Your book will be a collection of three short stories, one for each adventure.

4. Put your words and pictures in order. Then, add a title page for each adventure.

5. Write the words that go on each page, making sure to leave enough room for the picture.

6. Glue or tape your pictures to their matching pages.

7. Make a front and back cover for your book. Be sure to include the title and author (That's you!) on the front cover.

8. Staple your book together down the left side. Three staples should be enough.

9. Share your book with friends and family.

© Carson-Dellosa

Summer Adventures Picture Book
Finished Product Examples

The first story in a book usually starts on the right-hand page. This author also included a copyright page just for fun. She made her name into the name of a publishing company.

The author started her story by summarizing some events. Then, she grabbed the reader's attention with a hint that something exciting was about to happen.

© Carson-Dellosa

Labor Day

In the United States, Labor Day is celebrated on the first Monday of September. It is a day to honor the workers in this country who help to make it strong. For example, workers build cities, make products, keep people healthy, and teach children.

Think about the work you would like to be honored for doing someday. Draw a picture of yourself doing that work.

BONUS

Second-Grade Goals

Make sure you have the best possible year in second grade! Set goals for the new school year and work toward achieving them.

What skills would you like to make progress in by the end of the year? Are you shy about asking questions? If so, set a goal to ask at least one question per day. Do you love to read? Set a reading goal. How many books can you read each week? Maybe you have a hard time staying organized. A good goal might be to clear out your backpack every night before bed.

List your second-grade goals here. Then, check back during the school year to track your success! As you meet your goal each month, put a checkmark in one of the small boxes. At the end of the year, you can draw a star in the big box to show you met your goal for the school year.

Goal 1 _____

| 1 | 2 | 3 | 4 | 5 | 6 | 7 | 8 | 9 | |

Goal 2 _____

| 1 | 2 | 3 | 4 | 5 | 6 | 7 | 8 | 9 | |

Goal 3 _____

| 1 | 2 | 3 | 4 | 5 | 6 | 7 | 8 | 9 | |

© Carson-Dellosa

Answer Key

Page 3

Treasure Hunt, Step 1

Put your skills to the test! In this exploration, you will use what you learned last school year to design a treasure hunt. After reviewing your first-grade skills, you will hide a "treasure" somewhere around your house and then write clues to lead someone to it. Each clue will lead to the next, and the last clue will lead to the treasure.

To get started, think about the types of questions that would work as clues. You want to ask things that will get your treasure hunter to move from one place to another. Questions with numbers for answers work well. For example, if you want your treasure hunter to take 10 steps, you could ask, "What is 20 minus 10?" There are other ways to get someone from place to place, too. You could ask about the setting of a story and send the treasure hunter to a similar spot in real life. You could have the treasure hunter look for a particular shape based on its features (e.g. "Find the shape that has three sides that you can see from the backyard.") or find an object from its definition (e.g. "Go to the place that is attached to the house and has a roof but no walls.") See how many different ways you can come up with to get your treasure hunter moving!

In the box, list as many different kinds of questions as you can think of. Be creative and have fun!

Answers will vary.

© Carson-Dellosa — 3

Page 4

Exercise Journal, Step 1

Summer is an active time. This month, keep track of the kinds of exercise you get. Are you swimming, jumping rope, running the bases, shooting basketball, or playing tag? What about carrying groceries or walking up the stairs? Keep track of what you do and how often you do it. Then, add something new to your "routine."

To get started, make an exercise chart. Put on the chart any physical activity you do on a regular basis. As the month goes on, you can add new exercises or ones you didn't think of. As you do each exercise, make a tally mark on the chart. (See the tally chart on page 6 for guidance.) Continue on a separate sheet of paper, if needed.

Name of Exercise	Number of Times
Answers will vary.	

© Carson-Dellosa — 4

Page 5

Add or subtract to solve each problem.

1. 5 + 2 = 7
2. 9 − 3 = 6
3. 10 − 1 = 9
4. 3 + 4 = 7
5. 6 + 2 = 8
6. 8 − 5 = 3
7. 9 − 5 = 4
8. 8 + 2 = 10
9. 7 − 3 = 4
10. 8 − 4 = 4
11. 5 + 5 = 10
12. 6 + 3 = 9
13. 10 − 8 = 2
14. 7 − 6 = 1
15. 4 + 5 = 9

Write the capital letters of the alphabet.

ABCDEFGHIJKLMNO
PQRSTUVWXYZ

© Carson-Dellosa — 5

Page 6

Use the data from the table to answer the questions.

	Knights	Dukes	Guards	Counts	Jesters
King Ludwig	𝍶𝍶 I	𝍶 IIII	𝍶𝍶𝍶𝍶 II	𝍶 𝍶 I	𝍶 𝍶 II
King Jonas	𝍶 IIII	𝍶 II	𝍶𝍶𝍶𝍶	𝍶 𝍶 III	𝍶𝍶𝍶 II

1. How many knights and dukes does King Jonas have? 15
2. How many more guards does King Ludwig have than King Jonas? 21
3. How many guards and jesters does King Ludwig have? 54
4. Who has 28 dukes and guards combined? King Jonas
5. Which king has fewer counts and jesters combined? King Ludwig
6. Who has fewer knights? King Jonas

© Carson-Dellosa — 6

Page 7

Complete each fact family.

1. Family: 1, 4, 5
   - 1 + 4 = 5
   - 4 + 1 = 5
   - 5 − 1 = 4
   - 5 − 4 = 1

2. Family: 3, 7, 10
   - 7 + 3 = 10
   - 3 + 7 = 10
   - 10 − 7 = 3
   - 10 − 3 = 7

3. Family: 4, 5, 9
   - 5 + 4 = 9
   - 4 + 5 = 9
   - 9 − 5 = 4
   - 9 − 4 = 5

Write the lowercase letters of the alphabet.

abcdefghijklmnopqr
stuvwxyz

CHARACTER CHECK: Today, when a family member asks you to do something, repeat the request to show you were listening. Example: "Okay, I'll put my toys away."

© Carson-Dellosa — 7

Page 8

Circle the word that matches each picture.

1. bog — (dog) — hog
2. (star) — far — car
3. (bat) — bit — bet
4. peg — pug — (pig)

Read each sentence. Circle each noun. A noun can be a person, place, or thing.

5. The smallest (child) won the (race).
6. The red (wagon) was full of (toys).
7. Did (Cara) share her (candy)?
8. Our (neighbors) have a (trampoline).
9. (Andy) rode his new (bike) today.

© Carson-Dellosa — 8

Answer Key

Treasure Hunt, Step 2

It's time to gather the facts for your treasure hunt! Return to your list of question types on page 3. As you review your math and language arts skills, be on the lookout for questions that match the types on your list. Be open to other kinds of questions, too. Remember, you want to use questions that have clear answers that could take your treasure hunter one step closer to the treasure. Either copy questions directly from the workbook, or change them into what works for you. Include the answers, too—check the answer key to make sure your answers are correct.

Answers will vary.

© Carson-Dellosa **9**

Complete each fact family.

1. Family: 4, 3, 7

$4 + 3 = 7$
$3 + 4 = 7$
$7 - 3 = 4$
$7 - 4 = 3$

2. Family: 6, 3, 9

$6 + 3 = 9$
$3 + 6 = 9$
$9 - 6 = 3$
$9 - 3 = 6$

3. Family: 3, 5, 8

$3 + 5 = 8$
$5 + 3 = 8$
$8 - 3 = 5$
$8 - 5 = 3$

Say the name of each picture. Write the letter of each long vowel sound.

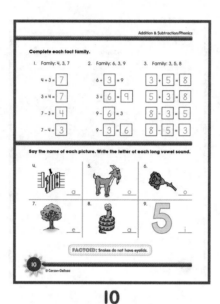

4. a
5. o
6. o
7. e
8. a
9. i

FACTOID: Snakes do not have eyelids.

© Carson-Dellosa **10**

Write > or < to compare each set of numbers.

1. 17 > 13
2. 93 > 83
3. 51 < 75
4. 49 > 26
5. 31 > 27
6. 78 < 87
7. 21 > 19
8. 73 > 38
9. 46 < 94
10. 14 < 29
11. 62 > 26
12. 98 > 78
13. 88 < 100
14. 54 < 65
15. 50 > 49

Think of three ways to finish this sentence. Write your sentences on the lines.

I like my best friend because . . .

16.
17. Answers will vary.
18.

© Carson-Dellosa **11**

Read each noun in the box. Write it in the correct column.

Dogwood Elementary	weekend	mall
peanut	Ms. Crios	sister
Marcus	Wednesday	

Common Nouns	Proper Nouns
peanut	Dogwood Elementary
weekend	Marcus
mall	Ms. Crios
sister	Wednesday

Read each sentence. Draw a picture of your favorite sentence.

The dog chased the squirrel.
The girl hit the ball out of the park.
The boy raced his dad home.
The baby hugged her teddy bear.
The woman splashed in a puddle.

Pictures will vary.

© Carson-Dellosa **12**

Count the tens. Write each number. The first one is done for you.

1. 20
2. 40
3. 30
4. 50
5. 10
6. 60

Say the name of each picture. Write the letter of each vowel sound.

7. r a ke
8. f a n
9. dr u m
10. f o x
11. ch i n
12. m i ce

© Carson-Dellosa **13**

Add or subtract to solve each problem.

1. There are 8.
   There are 2.
   What is the sum? 10

2. There are 6.
   3 walk away.
   What is 6 minus 3? 3

3. I have 4.
   I buy 4 more.
   How many do I have now? 8

4. Ivan has 2.
   Helen has 5.
   How many more does Helen have? 3

5. There are 7.
   3 more come.
   How many in all? 10

© Carson-Dellosa **14**

© Carson-Dellosa

Answer Key

15

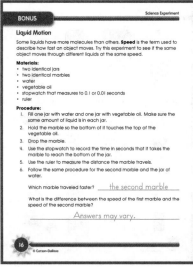

16

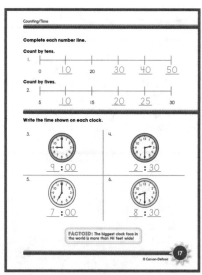

17

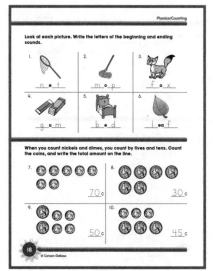

18

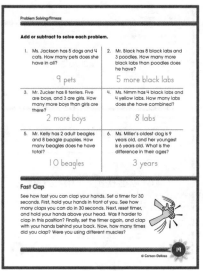

19

20

Answer Key

© Carson-Dellosa

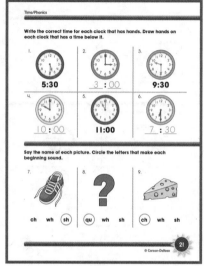

21

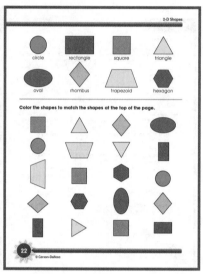

22

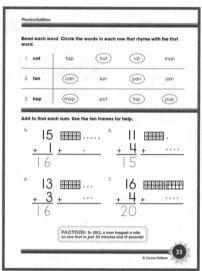

23

Use the picture graph to answer the questions.

🍇
🥕
🫑
🥬
🍓

🌱 = 1 seed

1. How many grape seeds are there? ___4___
2. How many carrot seeds are there? ___7___
3. Which plant has 9 seeds? ___strawberry___
4. How many more apple seeds are there than lettuce seeds? ___3___
5. How many strawberry and apple seeds are there? ___17___
6. Which plant has the fewest seeds? ___grape___
7. How many more carrot seeds than grape seeds are there? ___3___
8. How many apple and carrot seeds are there in all? ___15___

24

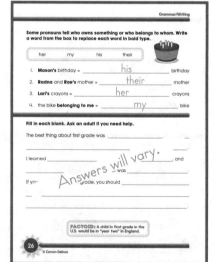

25

Some pronouns tell who owns something or who belongs to whom. Write a word from the box to replace each word in bold type.

| her | my | his | their |

1. **Mason's** birthday = ___his___ birthday
2. **Radna** and **Rae's** mother = ___their___ mother
3. **Lari's** crayons = ___her___ crayons
4. the bike **belonging to me** = ___my___ bike

Fill in each blank. Ask an adult if you need help.

The best thing about first grade was _____

_____

I learned _____ *Answers will vary.* and

If yo___ ___grade, you should _____

_____

FACTOID: A child in first grade in the U.S. would be in "year two" in England.

26

© Carson-Dellosa

Answer Key

Science Activity

Counting Beats

As you exercise, try charting your pulse rate. Use your index or pointer finger and your middle finger to take your pulse. Encourage everyone in your family who is exercising to fill out a chart, too.

Directions:
1. Give each person a copy of the pulse rate chart.
2. When you are ready to begin, have one person sit still. Find his/her pulse and start counting the beat for one minute. The timer watches the second hand of a clock or watch and says "Stop" after 60 seconds. Record the rate on the chart after the date and under the column marked **Before Exercise**. Do the same for everyone else.
3. Next, exercise. **After exercise**, take pulses as you did in Step 2. Mark charts.
4. Cool down by walking around slowly for one minute. Then, repeat Step 2 and record the pulse rate under **Recovery** on the same line.
5. Repeat three more times on three other dates.

Name:

Date	Before exercise	After exercise	Recovery
	Answers will vary.		

28

2-D Shapes

Draw each shape based on its description. Then, name the shape.

1. This closed shape has 4 equal sides and no slanted lines.

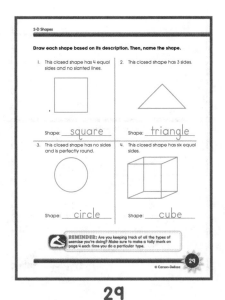

Shape: square

2. This closed shape has 3 sides.

Shape: triangle

3. This closed shape has no sides and is perfectly round.

Shape: circle

4. This closed shape has six equal sides.

Shape: cube

REMINDER: Are you keeping track of all the types of exercise you're doing? Make sure to make a tally mark on page 4 each time you do a particular type.

29

Addition & Subtraction/Grammar

Add or subtract to solve each problem. Use the number line to help you.

0 1 2 3 4 5 6 7 8 9 10 11 12 13 14 15 16 17 18 19 20

1.	3 +9 = 12	2.	7 +7 = 14	3.	16 −5 = 11	4.	12 −4 = 8	5.	6 +5 = 11

| 6. | 8 +8 = 16 | 7. | 19 −7 = 12 | 8. | 20 −3 = 17 | 9. | 14 +2 = 16 | 10. | 10 +5 = 15 |

| 11. | 18 −9 = 9 | 12. | 11 −4 = 7 | 13. | 9 +6 = 15 | 14. | 13 +7 = 20 | 15. | 20 −10 = 10 |

Underline the present-tense verb to complete each sentence.

16. Maria (left/leaves) for swim class in five minutes.
17. We (hopped/hop) on the bus when it arrives.
18. Please (turn/will turn) the lights off.
19. Do you (wanted/want/will want) to go to the soccer game?

30

Phonics/2-D Shapes

Say the name of each picture. Write 1 if the word has one syllable. Write 2 if the word has two syllables.

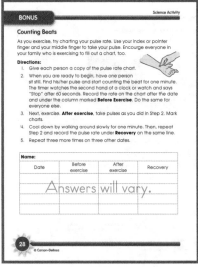

1. 1   2. 2   3. 2   4. 1

Draw the shape you have when you put the following shapes together.

5.   6.

7.   8.

31

Reading Comprehension

One of the characters below fits all of the clues in the poem. Circle the character.

Who's there? Was that the breeze? Or is something hiding behind those trees?

Who's there? The light is dim, but I don't think that you will swim.

Who's there? Did you hear me call? You don't look so very small.

Who's there? Can you fly? I see a tail going low and high.

Who's there? Come along! I see four legs, big and strong.

Who's there? Should I give you space? I see whiskers on your face.

Who's there? No, don't come back! I don't want to be your snack.

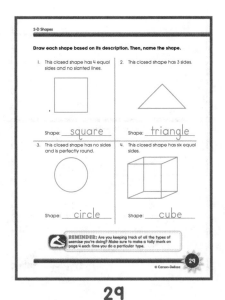

32

Partitioning Shapes/Grammar

Draw lines to show how you and a friend can equally share each item. The first one is done for you.

1.   Answers may vary.   2. SOAP

Draw lines to show how you and 3 friends can equally share each item.

3.   4.

Rewrite each sentence with a past-tense verb.

5. Clarice jogs to school.
   Clarice jogged to school.
6. Zach washes the car.
   Zach washed the car.
7. Sema sings beautifully.
   Sema sang beautifully.

33

© Carson-Dellosa

Answer Key

Solve each problem.

1. There are 20 🧢.
   There are 8 👟.
   What is the difference? 12

2. There are 7 🥄 on the table.
   There are 6 🥄 in the drawer.
   How many 🥄 in all? 13

Read each word. Then, find a word in the box that has the same long-vowel spelling. Write it on the line.

tie	goat	tweet	flow	day	peach

3. tree tweet
4. team peach
5. float goat
6. pie tie
7. bow flow
8. play day

34

Choose the correct name of each 3-D shape.

1. cone   square   (cube)
2. (rectangular prism)   cylinder   cube
3. triangular prism   (cone)   sphere
4. (cylinder)   rectangular prism   cone

For each sentence, write the future tense form of the verb given in parentheses.

5. Tomorrow, we (leave) will leave for vacation.
6. Our neighbor (take) will take our picture once the car is loaded.
7. When we get to the hotel, Mom (check) will check us in.
8. I (put) will put on my bathing suit right away.
9. My brother (cheer) will cheer when he sees the swimming pool.
10. The next morning, we (go) will go to the amusement park.

REMINDER: How many clues have you written for your hunt? Make sure you have both language arts and math questions.

35

Use the bar graph to answer the questions.

Batting Results

(bar graph: Number of Hits vs Jorge, Isabel, Kyla, Jackson)

1. Who got the most hits? Isabel
2. Who got the fewest hits? Jackson
3. Who got one hit less than Isabel? Jorge
4. How many hits did Jorgé and Jackson get altogether? 4
5. How man hits did the children get in all? 10

FITNESS FLASH: Lie down, stretch your arms above your head, and roll 10 times.

36

Add a verb to each subject to make a simple sentence.

1. The tiny brown puppy _____
2. Julie and Damara _____ outside.
3. The _____ around the flowers.

Answers will vary.

Draw the shape you have when you put the following shapes together.

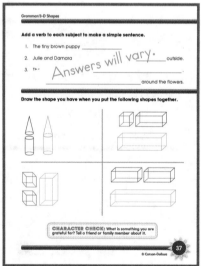

CHARACTER CHECK: What is something you are grateful for? Tell a friend or family member about it.

37

Exercise Journal, Step 2

Have you been keeping track of your exercises this month? Great! Now, it's time to add something new. Look at your exercise chart on page 4. Which exercises are the most fun? Highlight those and think about what makes them fun for you.

Then, use the box below to brainstorm ideas for a new fun way to be active. It could be an exercise you know about but haven't tried, a new version of a game like tag, or just a way to use your arm muscles while you walk the neighborhood.

After you've listed at least five ideas, choose your favorite one, and add it to the chart on page 4.

Answers will vary.

38

BONUS

In the Blink of an Eye

Did you know that people blink about once every 5 seconds? We blink in order to cleanse our eyes and keep them from drying out.

But, not everyone blinks the exact same number of times. The number of blinks varies from person to person and from situation to situation.

Test this out. Observe friends and family members of different ages. Try to watch some people indoors and some people outdoors. Using a stopwatch or a timer, record how many times each person blinks per minute. Are the numbers similar? Record your observations below.

Name	Blinks per Minute
Answers	will vary.

What do you notice about the data you collected? Did older and younger people blink at different rates? Did it seem to matter whether someone was indoors or outdoors? Do you think the number of blinks would change if it was a windy day? What about if the air was dusty or smoky?

39

© Carson-Dellosa

Answer Key

BONUS   Social Studies Activity

Symbols Replace Words

Symbols on a map show you where things are located.

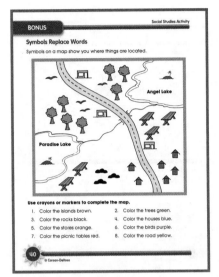

Use crayons or markers to complete the map.

1. Color the islands brown.
2. Color the trees green.
3. Color the rocks black.
4. Color the houses blue.
5. Color the stores orange.
6. Color the birds purple.
7. Color the picnic tables red.
8. Color the road yellow.

40   © Carson-Dellosa

40

Addition/Grammar

When you add three digits together, first add the first two numbers. Then, add the last number. Use this method to find each sum below. The first one is done for you.

1. 2
   7 9
   + 4 + 4
         13

2. 4
   4
   + 2 + 2
         11

3. 7
   2
   + 1 + 1
         10

4. 2
   3
   + 7 + 7
         12

5. 7
   + 6 + 6
         15

6. 8
   + 5 + 5
         17

7. 9
   + 4 + 4
         14

8. 7
   + 2 + 2
         17

Combine each pair of sentences into a compound sentence. Use the conjunction in parentheses ( ). Make sure to put a comma before each conjunction.

EXAMPLE: **Carter cleared the table. He didn't wash the dishes. (but)**
Carter cleared the table, but he didn't wash the dishes.

9. Janelle climbed the jungle gym. Audra went down the slide. (and)
Janelle climbed the jungle gym, and Audra went down the slide.

10. After lunch, Patrick rides his bike. He plays with friends. (or)
After lunch, Patrick rides his bike, or he plays with friends.

11. Mom saw the sand on our shoes. She knew we had been at the beach. (so)
Mom saw the sand on our shoes, so she knew we had been at the beach.

12. The dog sprinted across the park. Its owner sat down on a bench. (but)
The dog sprinted across the park, but its owner sat down on a bench.

41   © Carson-Dellosa

41

Reading Comprehension

Read the story below. Then, answer the questions.

Rebecca and Neela

Rebecca and Neela are best friends. They have the same haircut. They wear the same clothes. They love to read. Both girls have their own pet. Rebecca has a bird. Neela has a mouse. Rebecca lets her bird, Jade, fly around her room. Neela keeps her mouse, Julius, in his cage. Rebecca and Neela take good care of their pets.

1. What do Rebecca and Neela love to do? ___read___

2. How do the girls look alike? _They have the same haircut and wear the same clothes._

3. In the picture, what is one thing that is different about the girls? ____
Possible answers: different colored barrettes, different flowers on T-shirts; different hair colors; different pets

4. How do they play differently with their pets? _Rebecca lets her bird fly around, but Neela keeps her mouse in its cage._

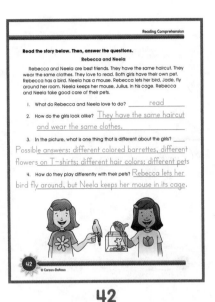

42   © Carson-Dellosa

42

Patterns/Phonics

Continue each pattern by drawing 3 more pictures.

1.
2.
3.

Say the name of each picture. Write the letters for the blend at the beginning of each word. In a blend, like sl in slide, two consonants make a sound together.

4. c l
5. f r
6. t r
7. g r
8. b l
9. s n

FACTOID: Frogs never close their eyes, not even when they sleep!

43

43

Representing Data

Skyler and his family went to the zoo. They saw 5 monkeys, 3 tigers, 4 giraffes, and 2 elephants. Color the graph to show how many of each animal Skyler's family saw.

Zoo Animals

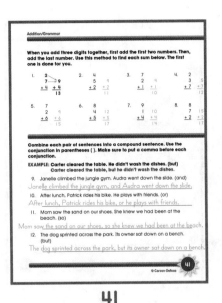

Skyler's family saw more ___monkeys___ than any other animal.

44   © Carson-Dellosa

44

Phonics/Number Relationships

Say the name of each picture. Write the letters for the digraph at the beginning or end of each word. In a digraph, like sh in show, two consonants together make one sound.

1. c h
2. q u
3. s h
4. w h
5. s h
6. l l

Write > or < to compare each set of numbers.

7. 21 < 23
8. 27 > 20
9. 98 > 89
10. 95 > 77
11. 53 > 41
12. 41 > 22
13. 14 < 18
14. 17 < 29
15. 57 < 76
16. 58 < 65
17. 74 > 39
18. 16 < 44
19. 37 > 28
20. 43 < 100
21. 72 < 81

45   © Carson-Dellosa

45

© Carson-Dellosa

Answer Key

Add to find each sum. You may need to carry a 1 to the tens place. The first problem is done for you.

1. 38 +4 = 42	2. 19 +6 = 25	3. 27 +5 = 32	4. 20 +6 = 26	5. 13 +4 = 17
6. 38 +8 = 46	7. 22 +6 = 28	8. 29 +3 = 32	9. 47 +2 = 49	10. 14 +1 = 15
11. 63 +5 = 68	12. 53 +6 = 59	13. 87 +2 = 89	14. 41 +4 = 45	15. 79 +9 = 88

Be Kind

How do you show kindness? Do you offer help when it's needed? Do you invite others to play with you and your friends? Think about a way you could be kind to another child. Draw a picture of what that would look like.

Pictures will vary.

46

Write a paragraph about your favorite exercise or physical activity. Give at least three reasons that this activity is your favorite.

Answers will vary.

FITNESS FLASH: Jog in place for 30 seconds, lifting your knees as high as you can.

47

Add to find each sum. You may need to carry a 1 to the tens place.

1. 63 +6 = 69	2. 42 +5 = 47	3. 29 +9 = 38	4. 71 +8 = 79	5. 62 +3 = 65
6. 45 +4 = 49	7. 19 +6 = 25	8. 30 +9 = 39	9. 16 +7 = 23	10. 22 +4 = 26
11. 30 +6 = 36	12. 81 +7 = 88	13. 47 +2 = 49	14. 56 +5 = 61	15. 48 +7 = 55

Add to each simple sentence to make a compound sentence. Use the conjunction and, but, or, or so. Make sure to put a comma before the conjunction.

16. Vanessa pitched the ball. _____

17. Dad bought the broccoli. _____

18. We want... _____ Answers will vary.
not start. _____

48

Write first, then, and last to show the order the pictures would happen in.

1.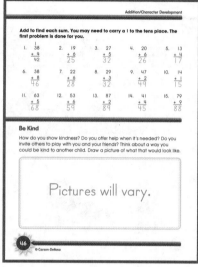
then   last   first

2.
then   first   last

Add to find each sum.

3. 15 +10 = 25	4. 19 +20 = 39	5. 23 +20 = 43	6. 31 +10 = 41	7. 47 +20 = 67
8. 13 +30 = 43	9. 29 +40 = 69	10. 17 +40 = 57	11. 11 +50 = 61	12. 60 +30 = 90
13. 75 +10 = 85	14. 50 +40 = 90	15. 25 +70 = 95	16. 42 +50 = 92	17. 12 +80 = 92

49

Say the name of each picture. Write the consonant blend at the beginning or end of each word. Choose from fl, gr, pl, sk, sm, and tr.

1. tr   2. sk   3. sm
4. fl   5. gr   6. pl

Look at each pattern. Draw the shape to answer each question.

7. What will the eighth shape be?

8. What will the tenth shape be?

9. What will the next shape be?

10. What will the seventh shape be?

50

Exercise Journal, Step 3

Now, take the exercise data you've been collecting on page 4 and represent it in a bar graph. This will help you see more clearly which exercises you've done most and least. If you need help, revisit the bar graphs on pages 36 and 44. Use the blank graph below, or create your own. After graphing your exercises, answer the question that follows.

Answers will vary.

Is what you do the most for exercise also what you like the most? If not, make a change for the better.

52

© Carson-Dellosa

Answer Key

Page 53

Social Studies Activity

BONUS

What You Need

People need certain things in order to stay healthy and safe. Circle the items below that are things people need, not just things they might want.

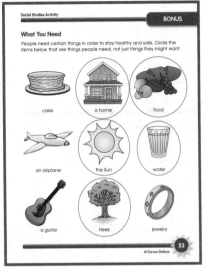

cake — a home — food
an airplane — the Sun — water
a guitar — trees — jewelry

53

Page 55

Phonics/Writing

Write the word that matches each set of clues.

EXAMPLE:
It begins like truck.
It rhymes with snap. → **trap**

1. It begins like star.
   It rhymes with mop. → **stop**
2. It begins like fog.
   It rhymes with sit. → **fit**
3. It begins like this.
   It rhymes with bat. → **that**

Write a paragraph for a younger brother, sister, cousin, or friend. Explain how to do something step by step. You could explain how to make a bed, ride a bike, or build a sand castle. Use sequence words like first, next, then, and last.

Answers will vary.

55

Page 56

Addition & Subtraction

Add or subtract to solve each problem.

#		#		#		#		#	
1. 17 + 4 = 21		2. 18 + 2 = 20		3. 12 + 3 = 15		4. 20 + 1 = 21		5. 19 + 6 = 25	
6. 14 + 10 = 24		7. 39 + 20 = 59		8. 42 + 30 = 72		9. 21 + 10 = 31		10. 18 + 30 = 48	
11. 60 − 30 = 30		12. 30 − 30 = 0		13. 90 − 20 = 70		14. 70 − 40 = 30		15. 20 − 10 = 10	
16. 80 − 50 = 30		17. 90 − 70 = 20		18. 50 − 20 = 30		19. 40 − 10 = 30		20. 80 − 60 = 20	
21. 12 + 3 + 2 = 17		22. 10 + 5 + 5 = 20		23. 14 + 2 + 3 = 19		24. 8 + 9 + 1 = 18		25. 4 + 7 + 6 = 17	
26. 3 + 2 + 1 = 6		27. 5 + 1 + 3 = 9		28. 4 + 4 + 2 = 10		29. 10 + 1 + 4 = 15		30. 11 + 2 + 2 = 15	

CHARACTER CHECK: Do you always keep your promises? Why is it important to do what you say you'll do?

56

Page 57

Reading Comprehension

Read the story. Then, follow the directions below.

Forest Animals

Many kinds of animals live in the forest. Some forest animals are very small. They have six legs. They are insects. Butterflies, ants, beetles, and bees are insects.

Some forest animals spend their entire lives in lakes or streams. They have scales. They breathe through gills. They are fish. Trout, bass, and catfish are fish.

Other forest animals are reptiles and amphibians. Amphibians spend part of their lives in the water and part of their lives on the land. Frogs and toads are amphibians. Snakes, lizards, and turtles are reptiles.

Look at the names of the animals in each list. Look at the titles in the box. Write the correct title on each line.

Amphibians	Reptiles	Insects	Fish

1. **Fish** — trout, bass
2. **Amphibians** — frogs, toads
3. **Insects** — butterflies, bees
4. **Reptiles** — snakes, lizards

57

Page 58

Writing/Subtraction

Write a paragraph describing what you see, hear, smell, and touch right now. Include what you taste, too, if appropriate.

Answers will vary.

Subtract to find each difference. Use the tens blocks for help.

1. 40 − 30 = 10
2. 30 − 20 = 10
3. 20 − 10 = 10
4. 40 − 20 = 20

58

Page 59

Grammar/Measurement

Write the correct punctuation mark at the end of each sentence. Use (.), (!), or (?).

1. This is the best day ever **!**
2. The car is in the garage **.**
3. Chickens cannot fly **.**
4. Where is my coat **?**
5. Is that your mom **?**
6. Watch out **!**
7. Why does water boil **?**
8. You can ride your bike **.**
9. Quick! Open the door **!**
10. Glue the yarn to the paper **.**

Use the paper clips to measure. Then, number the objects as follows: 1– long, 2 – medium, 3 – short.

3 — **4** paper clips
1 — **6** paper clips
2 — **5** paper clips

FACTOID: Chickens can't fly, but they can swim if they have to!

59

© Carson-Dellosa

Answer Key

© Carson-Dellosa

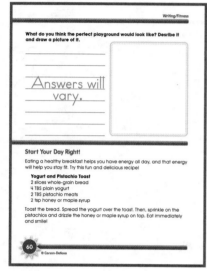

60

What do you think the perfect playground would look like? Desribe it and draw a picture of it.

Answers will vary.

Start Your Day Right!

Eating a healthy breakfast helps you have energy all day, and that energy will help you stay fit. Try this fun and delicious recipe!

Yogurt and Pistachio Toast
2 slices whole-grain bread
4 TBS plain yogurt
2 TBS pistachio meats
2 tsp honey or maple syrup

Toast the bread. Spread the yogurt over the toast. Then, sprinkle on the pistachios and drizzle the honey or maple syrup on top. Eat immediately and smile!

61

Follow the directions below.

1. Write a sentence that ends with a period (.).

2. Write a sentence th~~~ Answers will vary.

3. Write a se~~~~ ends with an exclamation point (!).

Count how many cubes long each toy is. Write the number on the line.

4.	5.	6.
7	7	6
7.	8.	9.
5	8	6

62

Add the word parts. Write the new word on the line.

1. walk + ed = walked
2. bright + er = brighter
3. un + button = unbutton
4. hand + ful = handful
5. re + name = rename
6. pre + test = pretest

Write the word or phrase that tells where each object is. Use under, in, and next to one time each.

7. The rake is _next to_ the tree.
8. Most of the leaves are _under_ the tree.
9. The cat is _in_ the tree.

FITNESS FLASH: Waddle like a duck across the room and back.

63

Read each paragraph. Read the sentences. Then, circle the main idea of each paragraph.

1. All insects have six legs. Butterflies and bees have six legs. They are insects. Spiders have eight legs. They are not insects.
   A. Spiders are not insects.
   B. Bees are insects.
   C. Insects have six legs. *(circled)*

2. Insects eat different things. Some insects eat plants. Caterpillars eat leaves. Bees and butterflies eat the nectar of flowers. Some insects eat other insects. Ladybugs eat aphids. Ant lions eat ants.
   A. Ladybugs eat aphids.
   B. Insects eat different things. *(circled)*
   C. Butterflies eat nectar.

3. Insects live in different kinds of homes. Bees build hives out of wax. Ants and termites build hills on the ground. Some insects, like mayflies and damselflies, live underwater. Other insects live under rocks or in old logs.
   A. Insects live in different kinds of homes. *(circled)*
   B. Some insects live underwater.
   C. Some insects build hills.

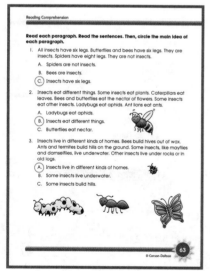

64

Circle the word that names each picture.

1.	2.	3.
hear / **hay**	**paint** / pant	**weed** / wed
4.	5.	6.
bet / **beet**	**light** / lit	**bean** / ben

Add or subtract to solve each problem.

7.	8.	9.	10.	11.
12 + 4 = 16	18 + 2 = 20	25 + 10 = 35	27 + 20 = 47	33 + 30 = 63

12.	13.	14.	15.	16.
70 − 30 = 40	60 − 60 = 0	30 − 20 = 10	50 − 40 = 10	80 − 10 = 70

17.	18.	19.	20.	21.
11 + 4 = 16	9 + 5 = 20	13 + 2 = 16	7 + 8 = 17	3 + 5 = 14

FACTOID: The first paints were made from charcoal or dirt mixed with animal fat.

70

Summer Fun Goal

What is one activity you would like to learn to do this summer? Think of a sport or hobby that would be fun for you to try. Then, plan how you will make it happen.

Summer Fun Goal: _____

What is the first step to reaching your goal? _____

Who can you ask for help? _____

What will be ~~Answers will vary.~~ ... for you? _____

What will be the hardest? _____

Draw a picture of yourself doing this activity.

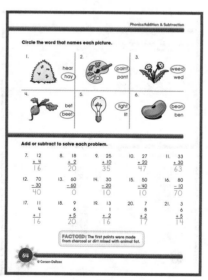

© Carson-Dellosa

Answer Key

Trip Planner, Step 1

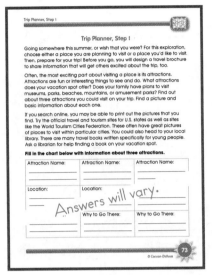

73

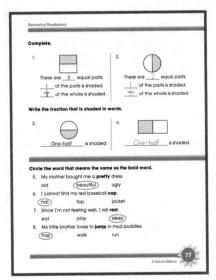

74

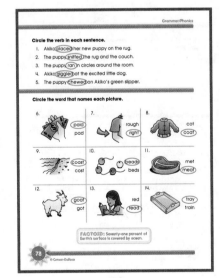

75

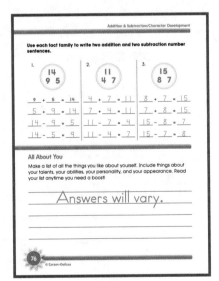

76

Geometry/Vocabulary

Complete.

1. There are __2__ equal parts.
   __1__ of the parts is shaded.
   $\frac{1}{4}$ of the whole is shaded.

2. There are __2__ equal parts.
   __1__ of the parts is shaded.
   $\frac{1}{4}$ of the whole is shaded.

Write the fraction that is shaded in words.

3. __One-half__ is shaded.

4. __One-half__ is shaded.

Circle the word that means the same as the bold word.

5. My mother bought me a **pretty** dress.
   old   (beautiful)   ugly

6. I cannot find my red baseball **cap**.
   (hat)   top   jacket

7. Since I'm not feeling well, I will **rest**.
   eat   play   (sleep)

8. My little brother loves to **jump** in mud puddles.
   (hop)   walk   run

77

Grammar/Phonics

Circle the verb in each sentence.

1. Akiko (placed) her new puppy on the rug.
2. The puppy (sniffed) the rug and the couch.
3. The puppy (ran) in circles around the room.
4. Akiko (giggled) at the excited little dog.
5. The puppy (chewed) on Akiko's green slipper.

Circle the word that names each picture.

6. (paid) / pad
7. rough / (right)
8. cot / (coat)
9. (coast) / cost
10. (beads) / beds
11. met / (meat)
12. (goat) / got
13. red / (read)
14. (tray) / train

FACTOID: Seventy-one percent of Earth's surface is covered by ocean.

78

© Carson-Dellosa

Answer Key

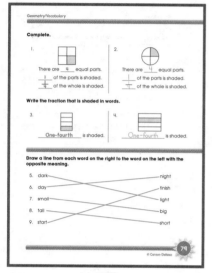

79

80

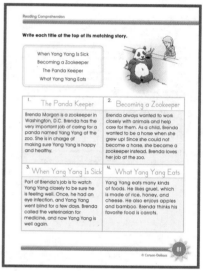

81

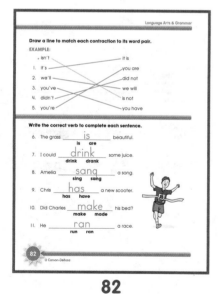

82

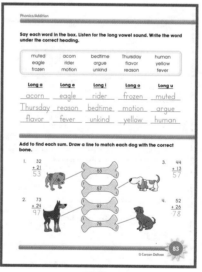

83

Reading Comprehension

Read each paragraph. Then, circle the main idea.

1. It was spring. The breeze was soft and warm. The grass on the hills was green. White clouds floated across the blue sky.
   A. The grass was green.
   B. The sky was blue.
   C. It was spring.

2. Noah went outside to play. His ball rolled near the fish pond. Noah had not looked at the pond since fall. He stopped to see the fish. There were four goldfish. There were also some new fish. They were small and dark. Noah ran back to his house to get his dad.
   A. Noah liked to play ball.
   B. Noah saw new fish in the pond.
   C. Noah had four goldfish.

3. Noah's dad came out to look at the new fish. He said they were not fish at all. He said they were tadpoles. He told Noah that the tadpoles would grow bigger and bigger. He said that in a month or two, they would grow legs. The tadpoles would grow up to be frogs.
   A. The new fish were tadpoles.
   B. The tadpoles would grow legs.
   C. Noah's dad put new fish in the pond.

FACTOID: Tadpoles have gills like fish so they can breathe underwater.

84

© Carson-Dellosa

Answer Key

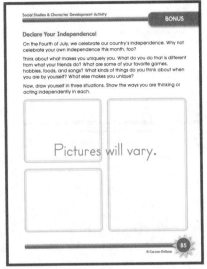

85

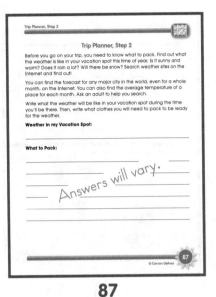

87

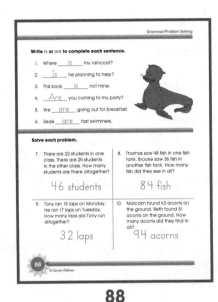

88

89

90

91

© Carson-Dellosa

Answer Key

Page 92 — Reading Comprehension

Read the passage. Then, follow the directions below.

Pretty Pancakes!

Butterflies are lovely to look at, but here is how to make one you can eat!

Materials:
- 2 frozen pancakes
- 1 banana
- 2 grapes
- 2 sausage links
- jelly or jam
- 2 toothpicks

Directions:
1. Toast two pancakes and cut them in half. Arrange the pieces on a plate to look like the four wings of a butterfly.
2. Peel the banana and place it on the plate. This will be the butterfly's body.
3. Spread jelly or jam on the "wings."
4. Use the toothpicks to hold the grapes like eyes on the banana.
5. Cook the sausage. Then, place it at the top of the banana as antennae.

Use details from the passage to fill in the missing words.
1. The __banana__ will make the butterfly's body.
2. The wings will be covered with __jelly or jam__.
3. Butterflies have four __wings__.
4. The antennae will be made from __sausage__.
5. A butterfly has two __eyes__ to see with.

92

Page 93 — Phonics/Place Value

Write each word from the box under the word that has the same vowel sound.

| boat | drove | box | job |
| rock | soap | chose | top |

home	cot
boat	rock
drove	box
soap	job
chose	top

Write the number and its expanded form.

1. 165
$100 + 60 + 5 = 165$

2. 178
$100 + 70 + 8 = 178$

3. 184
$100 + 80 + 4 = 184$

4. 158
$100 + 50 + 8 = 158$

93

Page 94 — Subtraction/Grammar

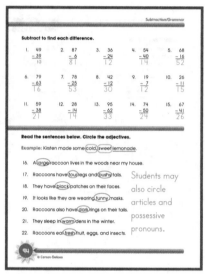

Subtract to find each difference.

1. 49 − 39 = 10
2. 87 − 6 = 81
3. 36 − 24 = 12
4. 54 − 40 = 14
5. 68 − 16 = 52
6. 79 − 63 = 16
7. 78 − 25 = 53
8. 42 − 12 = 30
9. 19 − 7 = 12
10. 26 − 11 = 15
11. 59 − 38 = 21
12. 28 − 14 = 14
13. 95 − 62 = 33
14. 74 − 50 = 24
15. 67 − 41 = 26

Read the sentences below. Circle the adjectives.

Example: Kirsten made some (cold,) (sweet) (lemonade.)

16. A (large) raccoon lives in the woods near my house.
17. Raccoons have (four) legs and (bushy) tails.
18. They have (black) patches on their faces.
19. It looks like they are wearing (funny) masks.
20. Raccoons also have (dark) rings on their tails.
21. They sleep in (warm) dens in the winter.
22. Raccoons eat (fresh) fruit, eggs, and insects.

Students may also circle articles and possessive pronouns.

94

Page 95 — 3-D Shapes/Language Arts

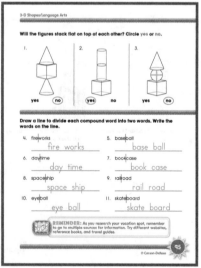

Will the figures stack flat on top of each other? Circle yes or no.

1. no
2. yes
3. no

Draw a line to divide each compound word into two words. Write the words on the line.

4. fireworks — fire works
5. baseball — base ball
6. daytime — day time
7. bookcase — book case
8. spaceship — space ship
9. railroad — rail road
10. eyeball — eye ball
11. skateboard — skate board

REMINDER: As you research your vacation spot, remember to go to multiple sources for information. Try different websites, reference books, and travel guides.

95

Page 96 — Writing/Place Value

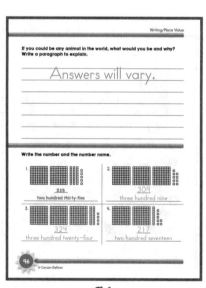

If you could be any animal in the world, what would you be and why? Write a paragraph to explain.

Answers will vary.

Write the number and the number name.

1. 235 — two hundred thirty-five
2. 309 — three hundred nine
3. 324 — three hundred twenty-four
4. 217 — two hundred seventeen

96

Page 97 — Social Studies Activity — BONUS

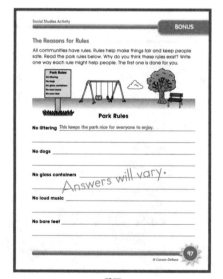

The Reasons for Rules

All communities have rules. Rules help make things fair and keep people safe. Read the park rules below. Why do you think these rules exist? Write one way each rule might help people. The first one is done for you.

Park Rules

No littering — This keeps the park nice for everyone to enjoy.

No dogs _____

No glass containers — Answers will vary.

No loud music _____

No bare feet _____

97

Answer Key

Page 99

Subtract to find each difference.

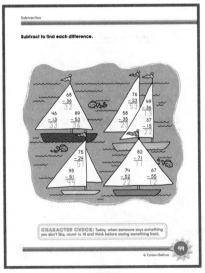

$$\begin{array}{r} 68 \\ -36 \\ \hline 32 \end{array}$$

$$\begin{array}{r} 46 \\ -13 \\ \hline 33 \end{array}$$

$$\begin{array}{r} 89 \\ -53 \\ \hline 36 \end{array}$$

$$\begin{array}{r} 76 \\ -23 \\ \hline 53 \end{array}$$

$$\begin{array}{r} 49 \\ -36 \\ \hline 13 \end{array}$$

$$\begin{array}{r} 58 \\ -35 \\ \hline 23 \end{array}$$

$$\begin{array}{r} 37 \\ -15 \\ \hline 22 \end{array}$$

$$\begin{array}{r} 75 \\ -24 \\ \hline 51 \end{array}$$

$$\begin{array}{r} 82 \\ -71 \\ \hline 11 \end{array}$$

$$\begin{array}{r} 95 \\ -51 \\ \hline 44 \end{array}$$

$$\begin{array}{r} 74 \\ -52 \\ \hline 22 \end{array}$$

$$\begin{array}{r} 67 \\ -55 \\ \hline 12 \end{array}$$

CHARACTER CHECK: Today, when someone says something you don't like, count to 10 and think before saying something back.

© Carson-Dellosa

99

Page 100

Use basic addition and subtraction facts to find each family's name. Then, write the name on the correct mailbox.

Moore 5   Hall 4   Nelson 9

1. The Moore Family

$8 + \boxed{5} = 13$

$\boxed{5} + 8 = 13$

$13 - 8 = \boxed{5}$

$13 - \boxed{5} = 8$

2. The Nelson Family

$7 + \boxed{9} = 16$

$\boxed{9} + 7 = 16$

$16 - 7 = \boxed{9}$

$16 - \boxed{9} = 7$

3. The Hall Family

$8 + \boxed{4} = 12$

$\boxed{4} + 8 = 12$

$12 - 8 = \boxed{4}$

$12 - \boxed{4} = 8$

Draw a line to match each word or phrase on the left with the correct pronoun on the right.

4. Jacob — he
5. the swing set — they
6. Eliza — it
7. Mom and Dad — she

© Carson-Dellosa

100

Page 101

Follow the directions below.

1. Write a sentence that describes an animal you have seen in the wild. Use two adjectives.

2. Where do ... *Answers will vary.* ... sentence that describes ... adjectives.

Follow the directions below.

3. Count by 5. Start at 600.

600, 605, **610** , **615** , **620**, 625, 630, **635**

4. Count by 10. Start at 350.

350, **360**, 370, **380** , **390**, 400, **410**, **420**

5. Count by 100. Start at 100.

100, **200**, 300, **400**, **500**, 600, **700**

6. Count backward by 100. Start at 900.

900, 800, **700** , **600** , 500, **400** , **300**

© Carson-Dellosa

101

Page 102

Write the numeral for each number word.

1.
- one — 1
- ten — 10
- six — 6
- four — 4

2.
- five — 5
- zero — 0
- eleven — 11
- seven — 7

3.
- three — 3
- fourteen — 14
- thirty — 30
- sixteen — 16

4.
- thirty-one — 31
- thirteen — 13
- forty-three — 43
- eighty-nine — 89

Be Enthusiastic

Think of something you do not normally enjoy doing. Maybe it's taking out the trash, cleaning your room, or loading the dishwasher. Now, find at least one way to make that activity fun. Can you make a game out of it? What if you sing while you work? Write your ideas on the lines below.

Answers will vary.

© Carson-Dellosa

102

Page 103

Say the name of each picture. Write oa, oo, or ow to complete each word.

1. s o a p
2. b o a t
3. f o o t
4. p o o l
5. m o o n
6. b o w l

Solve each problem.

7. The school play will have 14 tigers, 6 jaguars, and 16 lions. How many wild cats will there be in all? **36 wild cats**

8. There are 22 boys and 27 girls in the play. How many total children are in the play? **49 children**

9. Three dads and 16 moms are making costumes. How many parents are helping altogether? **19 parents**

10. The school sold 32 adult tickets and 68 child tickets. How many tickets did they sell combined? **100 tickets**

FACTOID: Tigers are the biggest cats on the planet.

© Carson-Dellosa

103

Page 104

Write the numeral for each number word.

1. six hundred ninety-six — 696
2. twenty-one — 21
3. eighty-seven — 87
4. ninety-seven — 97
5. three hundred sixty-two — 362
6. five hundred sixty-one — 561
7. seventy-nine — 79
8. fifty-four — 54
9. twenty-eight — 28
10. seven hundred sixty — 760
11. one hundred eighteen — 118
12. one thousand — 1,000

Make your bedroom sound like the most interesting place on Earth. Describe it in detail, using lots of bold adjectives.

Answers will vary.

© Carson-Dellosa

104

Answer Key

Read the story. Circle True if a sentence is true. Circle False if it is false.

Josh and the Bear

Josh heard something outside in the woods. It was still dark. Ma and Pa were sleeping. Josh lit the candle by his bed. There was no window in the little cabin. Josh went to the front door and looked out. Little dark eyes looked back at him. The little dark eyes were part of a big dark face.

Slam! Josh shut the door. He put the big wooden bar across it.

He ran over to the bed and shook his father. "Pa," he said. "Hurry! Bear!" He was too scared to say anything else.

Ma and Pa sat up in bed. Suddenly, they heard a polite knock on the door. Then, the bear began to sing. Josh peeked through the keyhole. He saw the bear juggling four apples. Josh couldn't believe his eyes!

1. Josh was afraid. (True) False
2. The thing at the door was a mountain lion. True (False)
3. Josh closed the door and put a wooden bar across it. (True) False
4. Josh was awake before Pa. (True) False
5. This story could have taken place a long time ago. (True) False
6. The story takes place at noon. True (False)
7. The story is very likely about a true event. True (False)

REMINDER: Have you been keeping an eye out for interesting animals? Remember to pay attention to what each animal is doing as you observe.

105

Read the sentences below. Write S if the sentence is a statement. Write Q if it is a question. Write E if it is an exclamation. Write C if it is a command.

1. _S_ Aidan looked at the treasure map.
2. _C_ Walk eleven paces in a straight line from the mailbox.
3. _C_ Take six huge steps toward the pond.
4. _S_ Aidan found an empty hole.
5. _E_ The treasure had disappeared!
6. _Q_ Who could have taken it?

Write odd or even.

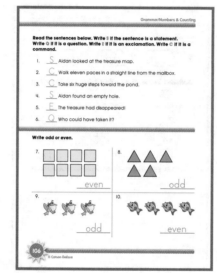

7. even
8. odd
9. odd
10. even

106

Classify your day into three groups: morning, afternoon, and evening. Write three activities that belong in each group.

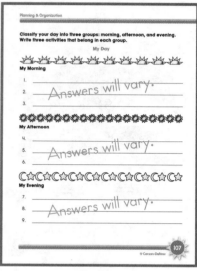

My Day

My Morning

1.
2. Answers will vary.
3.

My Afternoon

4.
5. Answers will vary.
6.

My Evening

7.
8. Answers will vary.
9.

107

Color the shape with the number that matches the description.

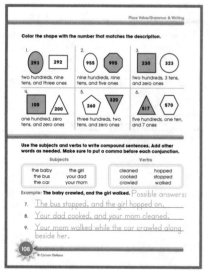

1. 293 292 — two hundreds, nine tens, and three ones
2. 955 995 — nine hundreds, nine tens, and five ones
3. 230 323 — two hundreds, 3 tens, and zero ones
4. 100 200 — one hundred, zero tens, and zero ones
5. 260 320 — three hundreds, two tens, and zero ones
6. 517 570 — five hundreds, one ten, and 7 ones

Use the subjects and verbs to write compound sentences. Add other words as needed. Make sure to put a comma before each conjunction.

Subjects		Verbs	
the baby	the girl	cleaned	hopped
the bus	your dad	cooked	stopped
the car	your mom	crawled	walked

Example: The baby crawled, and the girl walked. Possible answers:

7. The bus stopped, and the girl hopped on.
8. Your dad cooked, and your mom cleaned.
9. Your mom walked while the car crawled along beside her.

108

BONUS

Recycling Challenge

Collecting recycling is a great way to be a good citizen. Recycling used paper and containers means that these materials don't have to be made again from scratch. That saves energy! Recycling also keeps trash from traveling to faraway landfills, which means less air pollution from trucks and trains.

See how many recyclables you can collect in a week. Keep track of the number of paper, plastic, glass, and metal items. Make sure you rinse out any food or drink containers, and stay away from glass and metal containers with sharp or jagged edges. Finally, don't forget to either place your bin outside on recycling day or take it with an adult to a recycling center.

Put a tally mark in the appropriate column for every item you collect.

Paper	Plastic	Metal	Glass

Answers will vary.

109

Trip Planner, Step 3

If you're like most people, you want to know what the food is like where you're going. See what you can find out about what people eat in your vacation spot. Is the place known for any specific food?

For example, Philadelphia is know for its Philly cheese steaks, and Paris is known for its croissants. Find out what you should eat to get the full experience of the place you're visiting. Ask your family to help you find out what food the place is known for. Then, see if you can find some pictures of that food. If you're feeling really adventurous, ask an adult to help you cook something from that region!

List the foods you can expect to eat while on vacation. Be sure to include anything the place is specifically known for.

Answers will vary.

111

Answer Key

Adopt an Animal, Step 2

Now that you have a list of animals in the wild, choose the animal that you would most like to adopt. Think about these questions before you make your final decision:

- Which animal would be the easiest to take care of?
- Which would be the hardest to take care of?
- Which animal would be the most fun to play with?
- Where in the house would your new pet live?

Choose your favorite animal from your list, and draw it in your house.

Drawings will vary.

112

Adopt an Animal, Step 3

You want to be sure that your new pet will be happy and healthy. To do that, you'll need to find out everything you can about the animal you want to adopt. Find books at the library, or search the Internet for information on your chosen animal. Ask an adult for help finding websites with useful information.

NOTE: Since many wild animals are not recommended as pets, you may have to take your best guess about how to care for your chosen animal. Just base your guess on the information you find about how that animal lives.

Answer the questions below to prepare for bringing home your imaginary pet.

1. What food does it eat? _____
2. Does it sleep during the day or night? _____
3. How much space does it need to be comfortable? ___
   _____
4. How active is i~~t~~ ___
   Answers will vary.
5. ~~D~~oes it like to cuddle or have contact with other animals? Explain.
6. What is the biggest danger for this animal in your house? How will you keep your new pet safe?

113

Write i or e to show what sound the y makes in each word.

1. _i_ cry
2. _e_ pony
3. _e_ penny
4. _e_ twenty
5. _i_ try
6. _e_ city
7. _e_ baby
8. _e_ lady
9. _i_ fly
10. _e_ bunny
11. _i_ fry
12. _e_ jelly

Write how long each object is in inches.

13.
inches 1 2 3 4 5 6

14.
inches 1 2
___6___ inches

15.
inches 1 2 3

___2___ inches   ___3___ inches

CHARACTER CHECK: You can be kind even when you disagree with someone. What are some kind ways to say you don't agree?

114

Read the story. Then, follow the directions below.

A Great Castle!

Jessica and Alex are building a castle. Jessica builds the walls with brown wooden squares. Alex adds the green triangle roof. Jessica balances the long yellow cylinder towers. Alex tops them with red cones. Jessica puts blue rectangles inside for beds. Alex builds a path with small orange cubes. At last they are finished. That is great teamwork!

Mark an X in each box to show which child used each shape.

Shapes	Jessica	Alex
triangles		X
rectangles	X	
squares	X	
cylinders	X	
cubes		X
cones		X

Draw the castle.

Drawings will vary.

115

Use context clues to make the best choice for each bold word's meaning. Circle your choice.

1. The blue paint turned a **pale** color when I added water to it.
   bright   (light)   bucket
2. My brother found a **blade** of grass on his shoe.
   (piece)   knife   wheel
3. Dad likes to relax on the **sofa** after he takes us swimming.
   bike   (couch)   stairs
4. Would you like a large or small **portion** of watermelon?
   drink   (slice)   picnic
5. Prairie dogs sit on **mounds** to help them see danger coming.
   their tails   (small hills)   mountains
6. The aquarium has many **rare** fish that would be hard to see anywhere else.
   (special)   slightly cooked   scary
7. The cowboy tried to **calm** the neighing horses after the loud thunder ended.
   (quiet)   move   anger

FACTOID: Prairie dogs are not dogs at all—they are members of the squirrel family!

116

Use the ruler to measure each line to the nearest centimeter. Then, write each length.

1 centimeter (cm)

1 2 3 4 5 6 7 8 9 10

1. = ___9___ centimeters
2. = ___10___ centimeters
3. = ___8___ centimeters
4. = ___3___ centimeters
5. = ___7___ centimeters

Use a ruler to measure the sides of each shape to the nearest centimeter. Then, add.

6. ___4___ + ___2___ + ___4___ + ___2___ = ___12___ cm
7. ___5___ + ___5___ + ___8___ = ___18___ cm
8. ___5___ + ___1___ + ___5___ + ___1___ = ___12___ cm

117

© Carson-Dellosa

Answer Key

Use context clues in each description to help you choose the meaning of the bold word. Circle your choice.

1. It was a **pleasant** day. The sky was blue and the sun was warm. We put on our swimsuits. We ran down to the beach.

   dull   (nice)   sad

2. It was hot outside. Toby went to gather some eggs. All of the hens were asleep **beneath** the porch.

   (under)   above   with

3. Irma fell down in the yard during lunch. She hurt her arm. The **ache** got worse when she carried a big box for Mrs. Wilson.

   dream   page   (pain)

4. Some dinosaurs were small, but brachiosaurs were **huge**.

   fast   (big)   old

Use a ruler to measure each object to the nearest centimeter.

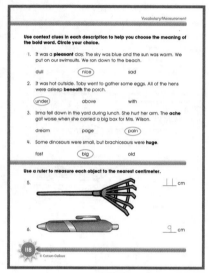

5. 11 cm

6. 9 cm

118

Describe the perfect vacation spot. Help the reader to see, hear, smell, taste, and feel what it's like to be there.

Answers will vary.

Write the correct punctuation mark at the end of each sentence. Use (.), (!), or (?).

1. Are we going to the game ?
2. Look out for the ball !
3. You are so amazing !
4. Are reindeer real animals ?
5. The girl on the swing is my sister .

FITNESS FLASH: March around the house or yard for 2 minutes. Try singing to the rhythm of your feet!

119

Answer the questions about the passage on page 120.

1. What is the main idea?
   - (A) Germs are things you do not want to share.
   - B. You can't see germs.
   - C. Wash your hands often.

2. Put an X next to the ways you can keep germs to yourself.
   - _X_ Wash your hands with soap.
   - ___ Stay away from animals.
   - _X_ Cover your mouth when you cough or sneeze.
   - ___ Get plenty of sleep.
   - ___ Eat healthy meals.

3. Put a T next to the sentences that are true. Put an F next to the sentences that are false.
   - _T_ Germs can make you sick.
   - _F_ Germs cannot get in your body through the nose, mouth, eyes, and cuts in the skin.
   - _T_ Cover your mouth when you cough or sneeze to keep germs to yourself.

Circle the correct short vowel.

4. Germs can make you s ___ ck.
   (i)   o

5. Germs get in the body through c ___ ts in the skin.
   a   (u)

6. Cover your mo ___ th when you cough.
   o   (u)

7. Get l ___ ts of fresh air.
   o   (o)

Use the dictionary entry below to answer the questions.

germ (jûrm), n. 1. a disease-producing microbe. 2. a bud or seed.

8. What part of speech is *germ*?
   noun

9. Use the word *germ* in a sentence.
   Answer will vary.

121

Complete each table.

Subtract 6	
9	3
6	0
11	5
10	4
12	6
8	2

Subtract 4	
7	3
9	5
10	6
8	4
6	2
13	9

Subtract 5	
11	6
7	2
14	9
5	0
8	3
12	7

Say the name of each picture. Write the vowels to complete each word.

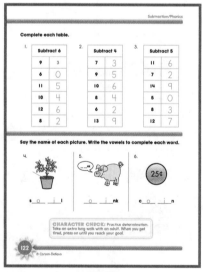

4. s o i l

5. o i nk

6. c o i n

CHARACTER CHECK: Practice determination. Take an extra long walk with an adult. When you get tired, press on until you reach your goal.

122

BONUS

Time To Go Home

This map shows routes the dinosaur can take to get to its cave. Use the key to find each symbol on the map. Then, follow the directions.

Dinosaur Cave Map

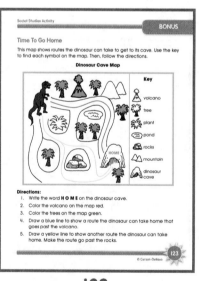

Key
- volcano
- tree
- plant
- pond
- rocks
- mountain
- dinosaur cave

Directions:
1. Write the word **HOME** on the dinosaur cave.
2. Color the volcano on the map red.
3. Color the trees on the map green.
4. Draw a blue line to show a route the dinosaur can take home that goes past the volcano.
5. Draw a yellow line to show another route the dinosaur can take home. Make the route go past the rocks.

123

Write the time shown on each clock.

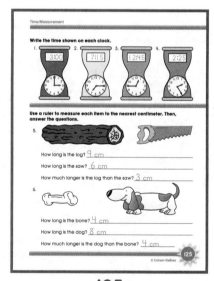

1. 3:00   2. 7:15   3. 12:45   4. 2:25

Use a ruler to measure each item to the nearest centimeter. Then, answer the questions.

5. How long is the log? 9 cm
   How long is the saw? 6 cm
   How much longer is the log than the saw? 3 cm

6. How long is the bone? 4 cm
   How long is the dog? 8 cm
   How much longer is the dog than the bone? 4 cm

125

Answer Key

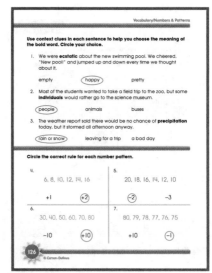

Use context clues in each sentence to help you choose the meaning of the bold word. Circle your choice.

1. We were **ecstatic** about the new swimming pool. We cheered, "New pool!" and jumped up and down every time we thought about it.

   empty   (happy)   pretty

2. Most of the students wanted to take a field trip to the zoo, but some **individuals** would rather go to the science museum.

   (people)   animals   buses

3. The weather report said there would be no chance of **precipitation** today, but it stormed all afternoon anyway.

   (rain or snow)   leaving for a trip   a bad day

Circle the correct rule for each number pattern.

4. 6, 8, 10, 12, 14, 16	5. 20, 18, 16, 14, 12, 10
+1 (+2)	(−2) −3
6. 30, 40, 50, 60, 70, 80	7. 80, 79, 78, 77, 76, 75
−10 (+10)	+10 (−1)

126

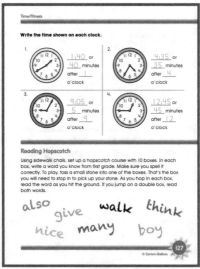

Write the time shown on each clock.

1. 1:40 or 40 minutes after 1 o'clock
2. 4:35 or 35 minutes after 4 o'clock
3. 9:05 or 5 minutes after 9 o'clock
4. 12:45 or 45 minutes after 12 o'clock

Reading Hopscotch

Using sidewalk chalk, set up a hopscotch course with 10 boxes. In each box, write a word you know from first grade. Make sure you spell it correctly. To play, toss a small stone into one of the boxes. That's the box you will need to stop in to pick up your stone. As you hop in each box, read the word as you hit the ground. If you jump on a double box, read both words.

also   give   walk   think
nice   many   boy

127

Circle the word in each row that does not belong.

1. scissors   (carrot)   books   paper   pencils
2. train   jet   (leg)   car   boat
3. cat   dog   (green)   fish   bird
4. lake   ocean   pond   (chair)   river
5. (bear)   apple   orange   peach   plum
6. Jane   Kathy   (Tom)   Jill   Ann
7. park   (scared)   library   school   home
8. tulip   daffodil   rose   daisy   (basket)

Use the unfinished sentence below to start a story. Use your imagination and be as descriptive as possible.

Under the stairs in a small green basket is . . .

Answers will vary.

128

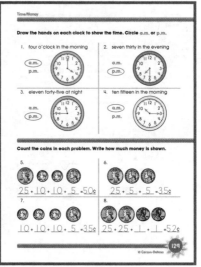

Draw the hands on each clock to show the time. Circle a.m. or p.m.

1. four o'clock in the morning — (a.m.) / p.m.
2. seven thirty in the evening — a.m. / (p.m.)
3. eleven forty-five at night — a.m. / (p.m.)
4. ten fifteen in the morning — (a.m.) / p.m.

Count the coins in each problem. Write how much money is shown.

5. 25 + 10 + 10 + 5 = 50¢
6. 25 + 5 + 5 = 35¢
7. 10 + 10 + 10 + 5 = 35¢
8. 25 + 25 + 1 + 1 = 52¢

129

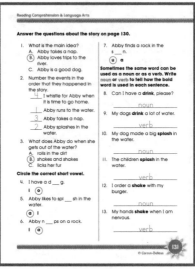

Answer the questions about the story on page 130.

1. What is the main idea?
   A. Abby takes a nap.
   (B.) Abby loves trips to the river.
   C. Abby is a good dog.

2. Number the events in the order that they happened in the story.
   4 I whistle for Abby when it is time to go home.
   1 Abby runs to the water.
   3 Abby takes a nap.
   2 Abby splashes in the water.

3. What does Abby do when she gets out of the water?
   A. rolls in the dirt
   (B.) shakes and shakes
   C. licks her fur

Circle the correct short vowel.

4. I have a d __ g.   i (o)
5. Abby likes to spl __ sh in the water.   (a) i
6. Abby n __ ps on a rock.   i (a)

7. Abby finds a rock in the s __ n.   (u) a

Sometimes the same word can be used as a noun or as a verb. Write noun or verb to tell how the bold word is used in each sentence.

8. Can I have a **drink**, please?   noun
9. My dogs **drink** a lot of water.   verb
10. My dog made a big **splash** in the water.   noun
11. The children **splash** in the water.   verb
12. I order a **shake** with my burger.   noun
13. My hands **shake** when I am nervous.   verb

131

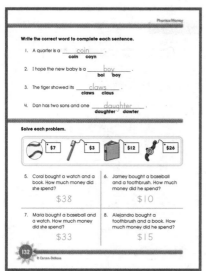

Write the correct word to complete each sentence.

1. A quarter is a coin.   **coin**   coyn
2. I hope the new baby is a boy.   bol   **boy**
3. The tiger showed its claws.   **claws**   claus
4. Dan has two sons and one daughter.   **daughter**   dawter

Solve each problem.

$7 $3 $12 $26

5. Coral bought a watch and a book. How much money did she spend? $38
6. Jamey bought a baseball and a toothbrush. How much money did he spend? $10
7. Maria bought a baseball and a watch. How much money did she spend? $33
8. Alejandro bought a toothbrush and a book. How much money did he spend? $15

132

© Carson-Dellosa

Answer Key

133

Which sport is the most popular with your friends and family? Ask each person to choose a favorite sport from the list. Make a tally mark beside each answer given. Then, color the boxes to graph your results.

volleyball _____   baseball _____

football _____   basketball _____

soccer _____   other _____

Favorite Sports

Answers will vary.

Sports: volleyball, football, soccer, baseball, basketball, other

Number of People: 0 1 2 3 4 5 6 7 8 9 10 11 12 13 14 15

FACTOID: The average volleyball player jumps up to 300 times in one match!

133

134

Use the sentence below to start a story. Use your imagination and be as descriptive as possible.

When you turn eight years old, something very interesting happens.

Answers will vary.

Answer the questions about ordinal numbers. Start counting from the left.

Grayson   Allie   Denise   Tanner   Lori   Matt   Rob

1. Who is third in line? Denise
2. Who is sixth in line? Matt
3. Who is seventh in line? Rob
4. Who is second in line? Allie
5. Who is fourth in line? Tanner

134

139

BONUS

Anchors Away

Solve the addition problems. Use the code to find the answer to this riddle:

What did the pirate have to do before every trip out to sea?

48	36	58	96	69	75	89	29
O	H	G	B	T	E	N	A

EXAMPLE:

42 +16	34 +41	60 + 9			17 +31	55 +34
58	75	69			48	89
G	E	T			O	N

26 +43	14 +22	52 +23			83 +13	24 +24	5 +24	52 +17
69	36	75			96	48	29	69
T	H	E			B	O	A	T!

139

140

BONUS

Space Words

Find and circle the space words in the puzzle below. The words go across and down. Use the word bank to help you.

Moon	Shuttle	Land	Orbit
Flight	Comet	Astronaut	Star
Rocket	Planet	Space	Sun

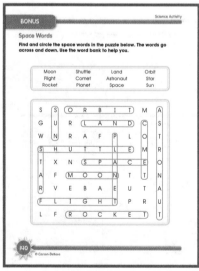

140

143

Summertime Song, Step I

Before going back to school, relive the summer! In this exploration, you will turn your favorite summer adventures into an original song!

To begin, think about all the fun things you have done this summer. Did you travel anywhere? Did you have a particularly fun day at the park? Did you sleep over at a friend's house? Make a list of your adventures. Is there anything else you would like to do before back-to-school? Put those on the list, too, and see if you can make them happen. Continue on a separate sheet of paper, if needed.

Summer Adventures

1.
2.
3. Answers will vary.
4.
5.
6.
7.
8.
9.
10.

143

144

Summer Adventures Picture Book, Step I

Use the fun things you do this summer to make a book about you! In this exploration, you will take or draw pictures of your summer adventures. Then, you will turn your favorite adventures into a picture book!

To begin, make a list of your favorite things to do in the summer. Maybe you like having picnics in the park, riding your bike in the neighborhood, or playing flashlight tag with friends. Include any favorite things you have done so far plus anything you would like to do before you go back to school. Continue on a separate sheet of paper, if needed.

Favorite Summer Activities

1.
2.
3. Answers will vary.
4.
5.
6.
7.
8.
9.
10.

144

© Carson-Dellosa

Answer Key

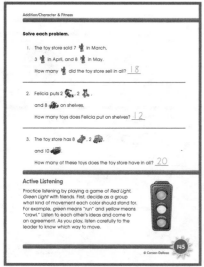

145

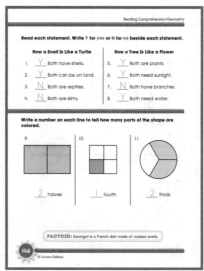

146

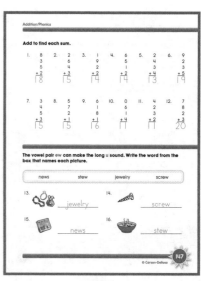

147

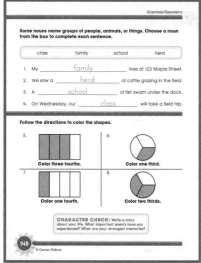

148

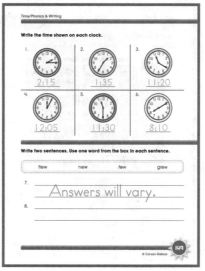

149

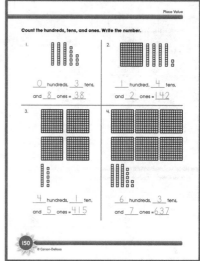

150

© Carson-Dellosa

Answer Key

Summer Adventures Picture Book, Step 2

Keep track of the fun things you do this month! Each time you do one of your favorite things, take a picture or draw something to represent your adventure. If possible, include a picture for the beginning, middle, and end of the event. Then, on this sheet, write a brief description of what you did. Continue on a separate sheet of paper. Also, if you would like, check items off your list of favorites on page 144 as you go.

1.
2.
3. Answers will vary.
4.
5.
6.
7.
8.
9.
10.

151

151

Write the time shown on each clock.

1. 6:25
2. 10:35
3. 12:15
4. 3:10
5. 9:45
6. 4:55

Look up the words in a dictionary. In each pair, circle the word that is misspelled. Write the word correctly on the line.

7. early ⟨thougt⟩ — thought
8. ⟨caterpiller⟩ scared — caterpillar
9. ⟨sents⟩ picnic — cents
10. because ⟨dragin⟩ — dragon
11. ⟨chane⟩ while — chain
12. ⟨speshal⟩ coat — special

FITNESS FLASH: Do 10 sit-ups. See if you can make each one last 5 seconds.

152

152

In each sentence below, circle the common nouns. Underline the proper nouns.

1. <u>Tasha</u> and <u>Sabrina</u> live on <u>Glenwood Avenue</u>.
2. Once, they had a ⟨colony⟩ of ⟨bats⟩ in the ⟨attic⟩.
3. Their ⟨neighbors⟩ <u>Nate</u>, <u>Bryan</u>, and <u>Nikki</u> live in the gray ⟨house⟩ across the ⟨street⟩.
4. They used to live in <u>Michigan</u> before they moved to <u>Maryland</u>.
5. <u>Nate</u>, <u>Nikki</u>, <u>Sabrina</u>, and <u>Tasha</u> take the ⟨bus⟩ to <u>Bellevue Elementary School</u>.

Use a ruler to measure each object to the nearest inch.

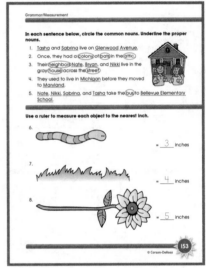

6. = _3_ inches
7. = _4_ inches
8. = _5_ inches

153

153

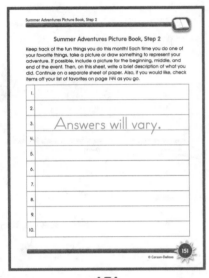

Use the calendars to answer each question.

April / **May**

1. Karina went to the dentist on the third Tuesday in April. What was the date?
   Tuesday, April _21_

2. Heath started his dance class on the first Monday in June. What was the date?
   Monday, June _1_

3. Today is April 10. Adam's family will see a play next Friday. On what date will they see a play?
   Friday, April _17_

4. How many days away is May 5 from April 29?
   6 days

What is the most exciting part about going back to school?

Answers will vary.

154

154

Social Studies Activity **BONUS**

A Walk Around Town

Let's take a walk around the town of Forest Grove. Use a marker or crayon to trace your route.

Directions:
1. Begin your walking tour at Forest Grove Inn.
2. Walk two blocks east to Elm Street.
3. Turn north on Elm Street. Walk to the Museum.
4. Go one-half block north to the corner of Elm and Lincoln.
5. Turn east on Lincoln. Walk until you come to the City Library.
6. Go south on Oak Street until you reach Washington Street.
7. Turn west on Washington and walk two and one-half blocks to the Burger Barn.
8. Lunch is over. Take the shortest way back to Forest Grove Inn.

155

155

BONUS Science Experiment

See the Light

The pupil plays an important role in eyesight—It is the opening in the eye, which lets in light. That light is then turned into images and sent through the optic nerve to the brain. If there is too much or too little light, the pictures in your brain will not turn out right. So, to stay in control over how much light gets in, your pupils get larger or smaller. Try this experiment to watch your pupils at work!

1. Turn off or dim any bright lights and look into a mirror. Draw your eyes, paying special attention to the size of your pupils.
2. Now, look at a light in the room for a count of 100. Then, draw your eyes again.
3. How did your pupils change from the first to the second step?

First Step	Second Step
Pictures will vary, but pupils should get smaller after looking at the light.	

156

156

Answer Key

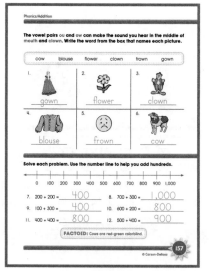

157

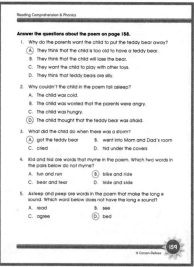

159

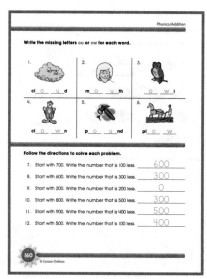

160

161

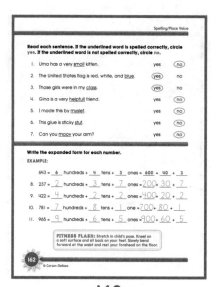

162

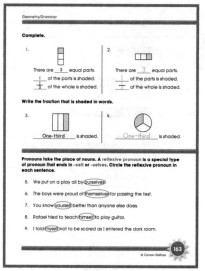

163

© Carson-Dellosa

Answer Key

164

Measurement/Number Relationships

Use a ruler to measure each branch to the nearest centimeter.

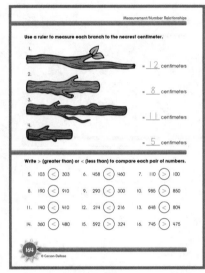

1. = __12__ centimeters
2. = __8__ centimeters
3. = __11__ centimeters
4. = __5__ centimeters

Write > (greater than) or < (less than) to compare each pair of numbers.

5. 103 < 303
6. 458 < 460
7. 110 > 100
8. 190 < 910
9. 290 < 300
10. 985 > 850
11. 140 < 410
12. 214 < 216
13. 648 < 804
14. 360 < 480
15. 592 > 324
16. 745 > 475

164
© Carson-Dellosa

165

Problem Solving/Grammar

Solve each problem.

EXAMPLE:
Case left for ball practice at 3:00.
His walk took 20 minutes.
What time did Case get to practice?
Think: 3:00 + 0:20 = 3:20

1. Ellen ate breakfast at 7:00. She ate a snack 2 hours later. What time did she eat her snack? **9:00**

2. This morning, Hau read for 15 minutes. He started at 9:00. What time did he finish reading? **9:15**

3. The movie lasted an hour and 30 minutes. It started at 6:00. What time did it end? **7:30**

4. Ellis left school at 3:30. He rode the bus for 30 minutes. What time did he get off of the bus? **4:00**

Circle each pronoun in the sentences below. Include reflexive pronouns.

5. Nate reminded (himself) to call Sabrina on Monday.
6. (He) needed to tell (her) about a club meeting.
7. (It) started at 4:00.
8. "(We) can walk there (ourselves)," (he) thought.

165
© Carson-Dellosa

166

Spelling/Patterns

Circle the word that is spelled correctly in each row.

1. do'nt — don'nt — (don't)
2. esy — (easy) — eazy
3. lauf — (laugh) — laff
4. (boys) — bois — boies
5. briht — (bright) — brigte
6. wonce — onse — (once)
7. (carry) — carey — carre
8. (hurt) — hirt — hert
9. (star) — stor — starr
10. peeple — (people) — peple

Continue each pattern by drawing 3 more pictures.

11. | 1 | 2 | 3 | 4 | 5 | 6 | 7 |
    | 2 | 4 | 6 | 8 | 10 | 12 | 14 |

12.

CHARACTER CHECK: Plan a schedule for the day. Write each hour down the left side of a sheet of paper. Then, write next to each hour what you plan to do at that time.

166
© Carson-Dellosa

167

Place Value/Writing

Use the hundreds, tens, and ones blocks to help you solve each problem.

1. 243
   + 126

    369

2. 542
   + 437

    979

3. 595
   - 222

    373

Write about a time when you felt proud. What made you feel that way?

Answers will vary.

167
© Carson-Dellosa

168

Reading Comprehension

Read the passage. Then, answer the questions.

Chemicals

Chemicals are everywhere. They make up our air, our houses, our food, and even our bodies. Chemicals help make everything different. They make apples sweet and lemons sour. They make leaves green in spring and red, orange, and yellow in fall.

When chemicals mix to form something new, it is called a *reaction*. As a banana ripens, it changes from green to yellow. This is from chemicals changing. When you mix chocolate with milk, you are watching chemicals change in a tasty way!

1. A good title for this passage would be:
   A. Chemicals in Our Bodies
   B. Why Bananas Change Color
   C. Chemicals Around Us

2. What is the main idea of first paragraph?
   A. Apples are sweet.
   B. Chemicals are everywhere.
   C. Leaves are green.

3. What is the main idea of second paragraph?
   A. Chemicals can cause changes.
   B. Bananas turn from green to yellow.
   C. Chocolate milk is tasty.

REMINDER: Did you write down activities you want to do before summer is over? Have you made any of those things happen?

168
© Carson-Dellosa

171

Addition

Write an addition equation to find the total number of items in each picture.

EXAMPLE: 3 + 3 + 3 + 3 = 12

1. 5 + 5 + 5 = 15
2. 3 + 3 + 3 = 9
3. 5 + 5 + 5 = 20
4. 4 + 4 + 4 + 4 + 4 + 4 = 24

171
© Carson-Dellosa

© Carson-Dellosa

Answer Key

Write the word from the box that names each picture.

| auto | yawn | stew | hood | faucet | fawn |
| laundry | screw | tooth | claw | book | moose |

1. tooth
2. faucet
3. yawn
4. screw
5. auto
6. book
7. claw
8. stew
9. moose
10. fawn
11. hood
12. laundry

172

Write the best adjective from the box to complete each sentence. An adjective is a word that describes a person, place, or thing.

| happy | fluffy | hard | pine | blue | nine |

1. His kite got caught in that _pine_ tree.
2. I cannot believe you ate _nine_ slices of watermelon.
3. Mom was so _happy_ to see us.
4. My tongue turned _blue_ from the cotton candy.
5. My pillow is very _hard_ and lumpy.
6. The rabbits all have soft and _fluffy_ fur.

Repeated addition problems help you get ready for multiplication. Add to find each sum.

7. 2 + 2 + 2 = 6
8. 3 + 3 + 3 = 9
9. 4 + 4 + 4 = 12
10. 5 + 5 + 5 = 15
11. 2 + 2 + 2 + 2 = 8
12. 3 + 3 + 3 + 3 = 12
13. 4 + 4 + 4 + 4 = 16
14. 5 + 5 + 5 + 5 = 20

173

Answer the questions about the passage on page 174. Read each phrase. If it describes Greg, write a G on the line. If it describes Tim, write a T on the line. If the phrase describes both boys, write a B on the line.

1. B is a twin
2. T has red hair
3. B plays catcher
4. G missing two front teeth
5. G has green eyes
6. Draw a picture of each boy.

> Pictures will vary.

7. What do you call twins that do not look exactly alike?
   fraternal twins
8. Circle the words below that have a long vowel sound.

twin   red   (base)
(teeth) (play) fun
(braces) Tim   (both)

175

Choose the adjective from the second column that best describes each noun in the first column. Write the letter of the adjective on the line. Some answers can be used twice.

1. the _d_ sunshine   a. green
2. the _c_ bird   b. rough
3. the _a_ grass   c. chirping
4. the _f_ squirrel   d. warm
5. the _b_ bark of the tree e. noisy
6. the _e_ lawnmower   f. furry

Pack Your Own Lunch!
Impress your family by making your own lunch! Try this recipe at home for a healthy yet delicious school lunch.

Mini Pizza Pitas
4 mini whole-wheat pitas (or one large pita, cut into triangles)
3 TBS pizza sauce
¼ cup shredded mozzarella cheese
Side of fruit

Carefully spoon pizza sauce into a small airtight container. Then, using a multi-sectioned plastic container, place the pitas in one section, cheese in another, and the side of fruit in the last. At lunchtime, assemble your mini pizzas, and enjoy!

178

Draw same-size squares ▢ to fill each rectangle. Then, count the number of squares.

1. 10 square units
2. 12 square units
3. 4 square units
4. 16 square units
5. 12 square units
6. 20 square units

Write the new word.

7. slide + ing = sliding
8. stretch + ing = stretching
9. move + ing = moving
10. snow + ing = snowing
11. make + ing = making
12. dry + ing = drying

REMINDER: Have you been doing any of your favorite summer activities? Make sure to keep track on page 151, and try to get pictures of the beginning, middle, and end of each event.

179

Circle the adverb in each sentence. Then, decide if the adverb tells when, where, or how. Write when, where, or how on the line beside the sentence.

1. (Yesterday,) it snowed. — when
2. Big flakes fell (gently) to the ground. — how
3. Ian looked (everywhere) for his mittens. — where
4. He (quickly) put on his boots and hat. — how
5. He opened the door and walked (outside.) — where
6. Ian (quietly) listened to the snow falling. — how

Complete each number pattern. Write the rule.

7. 6, 8, 10, 12, _14, 16, 18, 20, 22, 24_
   Rule: Add 2.
8. 20, 30, 40, _50, 60, 70, 80, 90, 100_
   Rule: Add 10.
9. 5, 10, 15, _20, 25, 30, 35, 40, 45_
   Rule: Add 5.
10. 6, 9, 12, 15, _18, 21, 24, 27, 30, 33_
    Rule: Add 3.

180

Answer Key

© Carson-Dellosa

Page 181

Measurement/Vocabulary

Use a ruler to measure the logs to the nearest inch. Then, show the measurements on the line plot. For each log, draw an X above the number that shows its measurement.

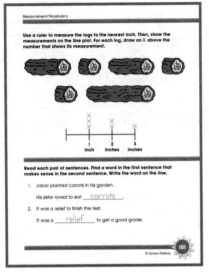

Read each pair of sentences. Find a word in the first sentence that makes sense in the second sentence. Write the word on the line.

1. Jabar planted carrots in his garden.

   His sister loved to eat _carrots_.

2. It was a relief to finish the test.

   It was a _relief_ to get a good grade.

181

Page 182

Geometry/Writing

Draw lines to divide each rectangle into rows and columns. Then, count how many squares there are. Write your answer on the line.

1. 4 rows
   5 columns

   How many squares? _20_

2. 3 rows
   4 columns

   How many squares? _12_

Use the unfinished sentence below to start a story. Use your imagination and be as descriptive as possible.

The door creaked slowly open, and I could see . . .

Answers will vary.

182

Page 183

Language Arts Extension Activity

BONUS

Write Your Own Ending

Read the story, and then decide how you want it to end.

Larry the Lion had been king of the grasslands for a very long time. But, the animals felt that they needed a new king. King Larry had become lazy, mean, and selfish. When King Larry learned of how the animals felt, he set them free and laughed to himself, "They will beg to have me back!" The animals did not beg to have Larry back, and so he moved away.

One lonely day, Larry found a mouse that was balancing on a branch over the river. He helped the mouse to the shore. Later, Larry found a baby zebra who was lost. Larry was kind and helped the little zebra find his home.

Directions:

Now, write your own ending to the story on a separate sheet of paper. What do you think happens next? Is the ending happy or sad? Then, draw a picture to go with your ending. Make it match the most important moment at the end of the story. Finally, give the story a title that fits.

Answers will vary.

183

Page 187

Reading Comprehension & Vocabulary

Answer the questions about the activity on page 186.

1. What is the main idea?
   - (A) how to play a game
   - B. how to run in a race
   - C. how to be in first place

2. Who goes first?
   - A. the owner of the game
   - B. the biggest person
   - (C) the youngest person

3. What is the object of the game?
   - A. to not trip when running a race
   - (B) to be the first to cross the finish line
   - C. to get the best start

4. What is the consequence of each action?
   - A. tripped on shoelace
     Go back 1 space.
   - B. getting tired
     Go back 3 spaces.
   - C. missed a hurdle
     Go back 2 spaces.

Read this game box. Answer the questions below.

A Rainbow Bridge Game

Hop to It!

The game that keeps you on your toes

For 3 or more players
For ages 5 to adult

5. What is the game's name?
   Hop to It!

6. How old do you need to be to play the game? _5 or older_

7. Can two people play the game? _no_

Write the base word for the following words:

8. tripped _trip_

9. running _run_

10. getting _get_

11. tired _tire_

12. crossed _cross_

187

Page 188

Addition & Subtraction/Vocabulary

Use the number line to help you solve each problem. Mark the number line to show your work.

1. 40 + 35 = _75_

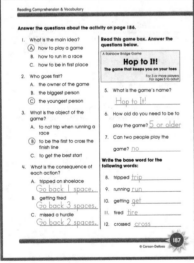

2. 80 − 50 = _30_

Use the words in the balloons one time each to complete the sentences.

smile   clown   balloons   laugh

3. My uncle's job is to be a circus _clown_.

4. He paints a big, red _smile_ on his face.

5. He makes animals by blowing up and tying _balloons_.

6. He goes to parties and makes children _laugh_.

FACTOID: One inch of rain can make about 10 inches of snow!

188

Page 189

Grammar/Measurement

Choose the correct adverb from the words in parentheses ( ). Write it in the blank.

1. Ian _quickly_ ran to his friend Ming's house. (quickly, quick)

2. He knocked _loudly_ at the back door. (loud, loudly)

3. Soon, Ming was ready to play in the snow. (Soon, Sooner)

4. Ming's brother, Jin, came home _early_. (early, earliest)

5. He _happily_ joined Ming and Ian in the yard. (happy, happily)

6. _Then_, they built a snowman. (Then, Last)

Use the mileage maps to answer the questions.

7. How many miles is it from Fairmont to Topsfield? _12_

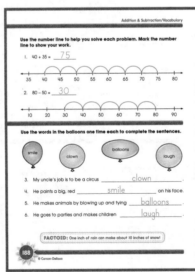

8. How many miles is it from Jackson to Lodi? _16_

189

Answer Key

Cross out the word that does not belong in each group.

1. apple banana ~~potato~~ watermelon	2. ~~whale~~ bobcat squirrel raccoon	3. boat car airplane ~~road~~	4. boots hat mittens ~~snowman~~
5. towel soap shampoo ~~shoes~~	6. cotton ~~rock~~ pillow feather	7. candle flashlight ~~mirror~~ lantern	8. bitter sour ~~lemon~~ sweet

Add or subtract to solve each problem.

9. 56 + 37 = 93
10. 48 + 35 = 83
11. 63 + 28 = 91
12. 88 + 12 = 100
13. 27 + 57 = 84
14. 59 + 28 = 87
15. 70 − 18 = 52
16. 81 − 22 = 59
17. 67 − 33 = 34
18. 54 − 17 = 37
19. 82 − 56 = 26
20. 71 − 38 = 33

190

Count the money for each problem. Write how much money is shown.

1. $1.42
2. $2.64

Use the words from the box to complete each analogy. An analogy is a way to show how things are alike. To complete an analogy, look at the first set of words. Decide how they are related. Apply that relationship to the second set of words.

EXAMPLE: *Finger : hand :: toe : _____*. (A *finger* is part of a *hand*. What is a *toe* a part of? The answer is *foot*.)

large	sky	square	ball

3. jump : rope :: toss : ball
4. three : triangle :: four : square
5. green : grass :: blue : sky
6. open : close :: small : large

FACTOID: If you jumped rope for an hour straight, your body would burn about half the calories you need for the day!

191

Use a ruler to measure the sides of each shape to the nearest inch. Then, add.

1. 2 + 2 + 2 + 2 = 8
2. 1 + 1 + 1 + 1 + 1 + 1 = 6

Read the table of contents. Write the chapter and page number of where you should begin looking for the answer to each question.

The Cool-Kids' Cookbook
Table of Contents

Chapter 1 Hot Breakfast	3
Chapter 2 Lunch on the Go	13
Chapter 3 What's for Dinner	21
Chapter 4 Snacks and Party Foods	35
Chapter 5 Delicious Desserts	49
Chapter 6 Fancy Drinks	57

3. How do you make scrambled eggs? Chapter 1 Page 3
4. What should I serve at my party? Chapter 4 Page 35
5. How long does a layer cake need to bake? Chapter 5 Page 49
6. What are some good picnic foods? Chapter 2 Page 13

192

Write a or an in front of each noun.

1. a career
2. an operation
3. a doctor
4. a scientist
5. an actor
6. an effort
7. an artist
8. a railroad

Use the prices for the snacks below to write each subtraction problem. Find the answer.

$2.38 $1.29 $1.38 $1.34

9. Mr. Smith bought a hot dog during the play. He paid with $3.00. How much change will he get?
$3.00 − $2.38 = $.62

10. How much more does popcorn cost than soda?
$1.38 − $1.29 = $.09

11. What is the difference in price between a hot dog and a soda?
$2.38 − $1.29 = $1.09

12. Erin bought a soda. She paid with $1.50. How much change will she get?
$1.50 − $1.29 = $.21

193

Add or subtract to solve each problem.

1. 66 + 24 = 90
2. 28 + 37 = 65
3. 73 + 18 = 91
4. 42 + 33 = 75
5. 19 + 54 = 73
6. 39 + 26 = 65
7. 42 − 28 = 14
8. 90 − 27 = 63
9. 44 − 22 = 22
10. 58 − 34 = 24
11. 74 − 36 = 38
12. 83 − 18 = 65

Write about something you did with your friends recently. Use at least two of these adverbs in your description: slowly, quickly, loudly, quietly, suddenly, before, later, after, sometimes.

Answers will vary.

FITNESS FLASH: See how fast you can move on all fours! Time yourself as you "run" from your bedroom to the front door.

194

Keegan wanted to know how many ants would come to a pile of sugar in five minutes. Each minute, he counted the number of ants at the sugar pile. Look at the graph to see Keegan's findings. Then, answer the questions.

Ants at the Sugar Pile

Minutes: One, Two, Three, Four, Five
Number of Ants: 5, 10, 15, 20, 25, 30

1. How many ants came to the sugar pile in the first minute? 3
2. How many ants arrived between the second and third minutes? 4
3. How many ants arrived between the fourth and fifth minutes? 11
4. How many ants had arrived by the fifth minute? 28
5. Between which two minutes did the most ants arrive? fourth and fifth
6. If Keegan had graphed the sixth minute, do you think the number of ants would have gone up or down? Explain. Answer will vary but should note that the number of ants increased every minute.

195

© Carson-Dellosa

Answer Key

Read the story. Then, follow the directions.

City Mouse, Country Mouse

Once upon a time, a city mouse went to visit her friend in the country. The country mouse spent the day gathering grain and dried pieces of corn in order to greet her friend with a nice meal. The city mouse was surprised to find her friend living in a cold tree stump and eating scraps. So, she invited the country mouse to visit her in the city. The country mouse agreed.

The country mouse could not believe her eyes when she arrived! Her friend lived in a warm hole behind the fireplace of a large home. She was even more surprised to find all of the fine foods that were left behind after a party the night before. The country mouse wished that she could live in the city as well.

Suddenly, the family's cat ran in and chased the two mice. He nearly caught the country mouse with his sharp claws. As the friends raced back to the mouse hole, the country mouse said, "I'm sorry, friend, but I would rather live a simple life eating corn and grain than live a fancy life in fear!" The country mouse went back home.

The two characters in this story are different from each other. Mark an X in each box to describe the correct mouse.

	City Mouse	Country Mouse
1. She feasted on fine foods.	X	
2. She would rather have a simple, safe life.		X
3. She gathered grain and corn.		X
4. She lived in a large house.	X	
5. She was surprised by all of the fine foods.		X
6. She lived in a warm place.	X	

FACTOID: A baby mouse is called a pinky.

196

Summertime Song, Step 3

You've had your adventures. You've made your drum. Now, it's time to choose the adventures you want to put to music!

First, go back to your list of summer adventures on page 143. Cross off anything that didn't happen yet this summer. Then, choose at least two events to use in your song. You might pick the events that were the most exciting or the most important to you. Or, you might choose things that scared you, made you laugh, or made you proud. Whatever you choose, make sure you have plenty to say about it.

Use the space below to write down all the important details you can remember about the adventures you want to sing about. Continue on a separate sheet of paper, if needed.

Answers will vary.

199

Summer Adventures Picture Book, Step 3

Return to this month's summer adventures on page 151, and review your list of favorite activities on page 144. Cross anything off the list that did not happen this summer. Then, choose three adventures to turn into a picture book. Which events give you the most to talk about? Which ones feel the most like a story? Choose those, and then answer the questions below. Continue on a separate sheet of paper, if needed.

Adventure 1: _____

What happened in the beginning? _____

What happened in the middle? _____

What happened in the end? _____

Adventure 2: _____

What happened in the beginning? _____

What happened in the middle? _____

What happened in the end? _____

Adventure 3: _____

What happened in the beginning? _____

What happened in the middle? _____

What happened in the end? _____

Answers will vary.

200

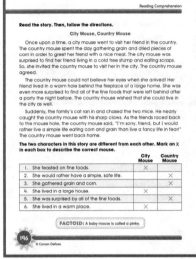

Add to find each sum.

1. $200 + 162 = 362$
2. $882 + 100 = 982$
3. $500 + 391 = 891$
4. $782 + 200 = 982$
5. $400 + 321 = 721$
6. $862 + 100 = 962$
7. $500 + 130 = 630$
8. $720 + 200 = 920$
9. $400 + 111 = 511$
10. $823 + 100 = 923$
11. $461 + 400 = 861$
12. $762 + 200 = 962$
13. $500 + 250 = 750$
14. $382 + 300 = 682$
15. $600 + 305 = 905$

Take Charge of Your Learning!

Think about one subject or skill you would like to improve in this year. Name three people who can help you do that.

Subject or Skill:

Who Can Help:

1. _____
2. _____
3. _____

Answers will vary.

201

Read the sentences. If the underlined word is an adjective, write adj. on the line. If it is an adverb, write adv. on the line.

1. adv _Yesterday_, Carlos and Grandpa walked to the pool.
2. adj The day was _hot_.
3. adj The _blue_ water was cool to touch.
4. adv Carlos and Grandpa _quickly_ jumped in the pool.
5. adj Carlos loved swimming in the _cool_ water.
6. adv Grandpa _easily_ swam a few laps.

Read each question. Circle the correct answer. Then, draw the shape in the box.

7. I have three sides and three angles. What am I?
   - A. a quadrilateral
   - **B. a triangle**
   - C. a hexagon

8. I am a quadrilateral with four equal sides. My opposite sides and opposite angles are equal. What am I?
   - **A. a rhombus**
   - B. a triangle
   - C. a pentagon

202

Subtract to find each difference.

YOU MADE IT!

$849 - 300 = 549$
$643 - 200 = 443$
$542 - 300 = 242$
$947 - 600 = 347$
$738 - 500 = 238$
$859 - 300 = 559$
$747 - 300 = 447$
$698 - 400 = 298$
$695 - 200 = 495$
$547 - 300 = 247$
$989 - 600 = 389$
$496 - 100 = 396$

START

CHARACTER CHECK: Write three ways your first day of school will be a success.

203

Answer Key

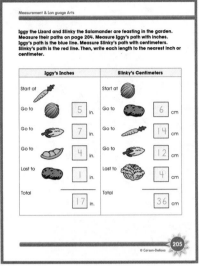

205

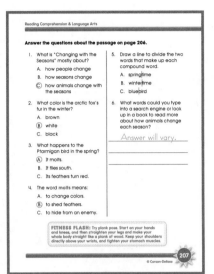

207

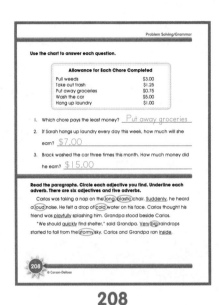

208

Page 209

Reading Comprehension/Addition & Subtraction

A glossary is found at the back of a book. It tells what certain words in the book mean. Use this glossary from a book about deserts to answer the questions.

captivity the keeping of animals someplace other than the wild
carnivore an animal that eats other animals
ecosystem all the living things in a certain place that depend on each other to survive
instincts ways of thinking or acting that an animal does not have to learn
stalk to creep up on an animal without being seen or heard

1. What does carnivore mean? <u>an animal that eats other animals</u>
2. A bird uses its <u>instincts</u> to build a nest.
3. Tigers and other cats <u>stalk</u> other animals.
4. What is an example of a place that keeps animals in captivity?
   <u>Possible answer: zoo</u>

Add or subtract to solve each problem.

5. 71 + 29 = 100
6. 76 + 12 = 88
7. 38 − 32 = 6
8. 92 − 75 = 17
9. 89 + 10 = 99
10. 583 − 400 = 183
11. 710 − 200 = 510
12. 582 + 400 = 982
13. 711 − 500 = 211
14. 712 − 100 = 612

209

Page 210

Problem Solving/Writing

Use what you know about money to solve each problem.

Zach has 3 quarters. Does he have enough to buy a book for 80¢?
He has <u>75</u>¢.   Yes   **No**

1. Tom has 2 quarters and 1 dime. Does he have enough money to buy a toy truck that costs 75¢?
He has <u>60</u>¢
Yes   **No**

2. Jane has 3 dimes and 4 nickels. Does she have enough money to buy a toy that costs 25¢?
She has <u>50</u>¢
Yes   No

Write a paragraph about your favorite book or movie. Include details about why it is your favorite. Your first sentence should include the title. Your last sentence should sum up your opinion.

<u>Answers will vary.</u>

210

Page 215

Social Studies Activity   **BONUS**

Labor Day

In the United States, Labor Day is celebrated on the first Monday of September. It is a day to honor the workers in this country who help to make it strong. For example, workers build cities, make products, keep people healthy, and teach children.

Think about the work you would like to be honored for doing someday. Draw a picture of yourself doing that work.

Pictures will vary.

215

© Carson-Dellosa

Notes

© Carson-Dellosa